SAVE SO I CAN
READ, TOO

Why the Left Is Not Right

Some Other Books by Ronald Nash

Choosing a College

Is Jesus the Only Savior?

Worldviews in Conflict

Faith and Reason

The Concept of God

Poverty and Wealth: Why Socialism Doesn't Work

The Closing of the American Heart:
What's Really Wrong With America's Schools

The Gospel and the Greeks

The Word of God and the Mind of Man

Freedom, Justice and the State

Why the Left Is Not Right

The Religious Left: Who They Are and What They Believe

Ronald H. Nash

ZondervanPublishingHouse
Grand Rapids, Michigan

A Division of HarperCollinsPublishers

Why the Left Is Not Right
Copyright © 1996 by Ronald H. Nash

Requests for information should be addressed to:

ZondervanPublishingHouse
Grand Rapids, Michigan 49530

Library of Congress Cataloging-in-Publication Data

Nash, Ronald H.
     Why the left is not right : the religious left—who they are and what they
believe / Ronald H. Nash.
       p.   cm.
     Includes bibliographical references.
     ISBN: 0-310-21015-1 (softcover)
     1. Liberalism (Religion)—United States—Controversial literature.
2. Liberalism (Religion)—Protestant churches—Controversial literature.
3. Liberalism (Religion)—Catholic churches—Controversial literature.
4. Christianity and politics—History—20th century.   5. Catholic church—
United States—History—20th century.   6. United States—Church
history—20th century.   7. United States—Politics and government—1993–
I. Title.
BR526.N28 1996
277.3'0825—dc20
                                     96-00000
                                        CIP

Permissions for quotations are cited in the Acknowledgments and in endnotes.

Printed in the United States of America

---

96 97 98 99 00 01 02✜ DH/ 10 9 8 7 6 5 4 3 2 1

To
Jeff, Cindy, Andrew, and Amanda

Contents

Acknowledgments

I wish to acknowledge help from several friends. Dr. Ron Taber of Olympia, Washington; Michael Cromartie of the Ethics and Public Policy Center in Washington, D.C.; and the Rev. William Haynes of Longwood, Florida, read early drafts of the book. Their comments and suggestions were very helpful. Tim Wehse, my student assistant at Reformed Theological Seminary, also read the manuscript and helped with important research. John Muether, Dan Wright, and Gary Graber of the RTS library were generous with their time and aided my research by securing material from other libraries.

I am grateful for permission to use extensive quotations from the following publications:

Freedom, Justice and Hope, edited by Marvin Olasky, copyright © 1988, excerpts from chapter 8. Used by permission of Good News Publishers/Crossway Books, Wheaton, Illinois 60187.

Politically Incorrect, Ralph Reed, copyright © 1994, Word, Inc., Dallas, Texas. All rights reserved.

Is Jesus a Republican or a Democrat?—and 14 Other Polarizing Issues, Tony Campolo, copyright © 1995, Word, Inc., Dallas, Texas. All rights reserved.

Chapter One

Is There a Religious Left?

It has become very hard to ignore all the talk these days about something called "the Religious Right." Most Americans have learned that this term refers to theologically conservative Protestants (often called evangelicals) who have supposedly ended years of absence from political activity by trying to "take over America." Such exaggerations and outright distortions have helped make "the Religious Right" label a highly prejudicial term that often carries negative connotations.

Many Americans associate the term "Religious Right" with television preachers such as Jerry Falwell and Pat Robertson. They may remember that Falwell once headed a now-defunct organization called the Moral Majority and that Robertson founded the Christian Coalition. But whoever Religious Right people may be, they get accused of more bad motives and nasty deeds than any group of villains in an old-time movie.

In the midst of the emotionally charged and pejorative talk about a Religious Right, it seems extremely odd that nobody ever talks about a Religious Left. It seems never to have occurred to some people that if there is a Religious Right, then there may be a Religious Left. If the Religious Left exists, why is there so little information about it? And who are the people who represent it, and what do they believe?

As this book's title suggests, there really is a Religious Left. There are many sources that provide partial information or pieces of the puzzle. At the moment, however, this is the only available book that provides a reasonably complete picture of the Religious Left.

Since the members of the particular segment of the Religious Left that I will be concentrating on have been around for thirty or more years, the little attention they have received as leftists is surprising. Why has there been such silence about the Religious Left? Why is it possible to search through newspapers, transcripts of television programs, and college lectures and find little or no mention of the Religious Left?

One plausible reason is that print and television journalists are themselves so liberal[1] that they either cannot see or cannot bring themselves to admit that people who think the way they do are part of "the Left." Sometimes even fully committed liberals do not want to be known as liberals. America's print and TV journalists refer to the most liberal members of the U.S. Congress as "moderates." Sometimes, it seems, there are *no* liberals in the American government—or elsewhere in society—if we are to believe the liberal, mainstream media. One might naively conclude that there are only two groups of politically active people in our country, the so-called moderates and everyone else—who must be not only right-wing but probably extremist, to boot. In this clever but ideologically manipulative way, the religious opponents of Christian conservatives are presented as moderates. This may be convenient for them, but it is also quite dishonest.

It is interesting to see that the members of the Religious Left that we will consider recently began to describe themselves as *moderates* and centrists. During the 1970s and 1980s, when their political heroes included George McGovern, Ted Kennedy, Walter Mondale, Howard Metzenbaum, and Michael Dukakis, these people proudly proclaimed their liberal or radical convictions. During the years when the heroes of some of these people included the Viet Cong, the army of North Vietnam, and later the Marxist Sandinistas of Nicaragua, they continued to describe themselves as liberals or radicals. But now these very same people describe themselves as centrists. In his bimonthly magazine, *Sojourners*, Jim Wallis currently describes himself and his followers with the phrase, "Not from the Left and not from the Right, but from the Spirit." Presumably, the Spirit Wallis has in mind is the Holy Spirit.

This new public face of moderation and centrism is very interesting. Why would people who have boasted of their left-wing views for at least two decades suddenly adopt a new public image? On our journey through this book, we may encounter some answers to this question.

WHAT RELIGIOUS LEFT ARE WE TALKING ABOUT?

At least three major groups of the Religious Left exist in the United States. One of these, itself a movement with numerous subdivisions, includes many of the clergy, denominational leaders, and academicians in America's largely liberal (in the theological sense) mainline denominations. A second branch of the Religious Left is composed of the growing number of politically liberal Roman Catholics in America. I discuss both groups in chapter 2.

It is the third branch of the Religious Left to which I will give the most attention. The group of people I have in mind are or profess to be theologically conservative Protestants—that is, evangelicals. In spite of their occasional theological differences with representatives of the Catholic and mainline Protestant Left, they find many areas of agreement, especially in political, economic, and social matters.

There are at least two reasons why this is the right time to undertake an assessment of the evangelical Left. The first is their recent return to prominence through the publication of a document titled *The Cry for Renewal* and attendant news conferences. These evangelicals have made it clear that their document is only the opening salvo in what they promise will be a flurry of activity on behalf of their cause.[2] A later chapter in this book will examine this document and report on critical reactions to it.

The second reason—and this is largely supposition at this point—is the interesting coincidence that the return of the evangelical Left to public attention occurred less than a year before the

start of the 1996 political campaign. As more and more evangelicals leave the Democratic Party and support conservative (i.e.,
Republican) candidates, President Clinton's advisors know that his
chances of reelection depend on his winning a minimum of 20
percent of the evangelical vote. While it may seem cynical, some
find it plausible to believe that one objective of at least some of the
evangelical Left is to keep Bill Clinton in office. Since President
Clinton has referred publicly to one member of the religious Left,
Tony Campolo, as his good friend,[3] the possibility of a hidden political agenda cannot be ignored. As we will see, electing liberals has
been a major objective of the evangelical Left.

There is a third reason for this book. The evangelical Left
have made clear their total opposition to conservative Christian
organizations such as the Christian Coalition. Their well-known
dislike for evangelicals Jerry Falwell, Pat Robertson, Ralph Reed,
and other conservative social activists has generated expected
interest from media liberals who are intrigued by and appreciative
of left-wing evangelicals whose arguments can be used to help
sway public opinion against the conservative cause.

THE EVANGELICAL LEFT: WHO ARE THEY?

The people who will receive most of my attention in this book are
(1) Jim Wallis, editor of *Sojourners* magazine and leader of a very
small community in Washington, D.C., that goes by the same
name; (2) Ronald Sider, the well-known and respected evangelical
author of such books as *Rich Christians in a World of Hunger*,
professor of theology and culture at Eastern Baptist Seminary in
Philadelphia, and the president of Evangelicals for Social Action
(ESA); and (3) Tony Campolo, a professor of sociology at Eastern
College, located in the Philadelphia suburb of St. Davids, and a
nationally known evangelical author and speaker who is also
active in humanitarian activities on behalf of the poor in several
countries, including Haiti.

Along the way I will have occasion to discuss or mention the
views of other members of the evangelical Left.

WHY SHOULD WE CARE?

Years ago, I suppose, many conservative Christians would have been surprised—even shocked—that self-professed evangelicals were supporting and even actively promoting liberal causes. But those were the days when evangelicals—better known as fundamentalists—separated themselves from societal affairs at large. One still occasionally encounters people like this. But most evangelicals today care deeply about what is happening in America's schools, government, and abortion clinics. They also care about racial justice, the environment, the poor, the elderly, and the homeless. As indicated by the charities they support, they also care about poor, sick, and starving people in other nations.

For most of my lifetime, liberals have been telling this nation that caring in these ways must translate into voting for liberal politicians and supporting liberal social policies. The evangelical liberals have been part of this liberal establishment. But I contend that liberalism is an exercise in fraud and deceit. The more than five trillion dollars of taxpayers' money the federal government spent in the vain hope that it would put an end to poverty in America did not simply fall short of the goal. It actually made the situation worse.[4] We now have more poor people in the United States than there were before the start of the War on Poverty programs in the mid-sixties—and they are also worse off today.

Some in the evangelical Left now tell us they no longer support the liberal welfare state. They admit that it has failed, and they propose to provide new leadership and direction in the next decade. The past record of these people needs to be known so we can better judge their claims about the present and their promises for the future. Why do they attack evangelical conservatives? What do they believe? Are they really centrists, and if not, why do they claim they are?

A WORD ABOUT RELIGIOUS CONSERVATIVES

The secular and religious Left find it convenient to demonize politically conservative Christians. It is true that many evangelicals were unconscionably inattentive to some social problems thirty or forty years ago; of course, the world was a different place back then.

Michael Cromartie of the Ethics and Public Policy Center in Washington, D.C., observes:

> It is strange that twentieth-century evangelical Christians would have ever needed to be convinced that they should be concerned about social problems. Many of their spiritual forebears always were. Their compassion and fervor animated the campaigns against the slave trade and child labor in England and, one could argue, was the basis of most reform initiatives of the early nineteenth century. The claims that the faith of American Christians should always be an intensely private affair between the individual and God would have been news to such diverse persons as the Pilgrims, from John Winthrop to Jonathan Edwards, Abraham Lincoln and the abolitionists of slavery.[5]

Whatever their shortcomings may have been back then, Michael Cromartie observes, "Evangelicals of every perspective no longer need convincing that political and social concern is an important part of Christian discipleship. It is a settled issue that 'the least of these' among us should be treated with both charity *and* justice. The debates now revolve around prudential questions regarding which policies are in fact the most effective in meeting the normative standards of justice."[6]

The members of the evangelical Left are wrong to claim that they hold the monopoly on concern for peace and justice. The more central issue for evangelicals today is what those terms mean. The evangelical Left has appeared to some to have simply assumed the standard liberal understanding of the words and then discredited anyone (including their politically conservative brethren) who understood the terms differently and who pursued the objectives of peace and justice in a different way.

There is no evidence to support liberal insinuations that being a conservative entails opposition to racial and social justice and means being unconcerned about unjust social structures or poverty. What the Left does is simply assume, for example, that concern for poverty *must* manifest itself in unqualified support for misguided liberal social programs. They simply take it for granted that concern for racial justice must translate into support for so-called Affirmative Action programs that turn out to be exercises in reverse discrimination.

It is time to strip away the false front that the evangelical Left has hidden behind and see what they really stand for.

THE STRUCTURE OF THE BOOK

A brief word about the organization of the book may be helpful. Chapter 2 examines the members of the Religious Left who belong denominationally to America's mainline Protestant churches or are part of American Catholicism. Chapters 3 and 4 examine vital background issues, especially the attachment of many in the Religious Left to Marxist (or Marxist-sounding) ideas. Especially important, I think, is the link between many in the Religious Left today and radical political movements of thirty years ago such as the New Left.

The next six chapters center on three representatives of the evangelical Left, each serving as models of somewhat different beliefs, attitudes, and interests. Since these three persons—Jim Wallis, Ronald Sider, and Tony Campolo—have been the driving force behind much evangelical Left activity, my focus on them seems justified.

The remaining chapters in the book explore other issues that make possible some comparisons between the evangelical Left and more conservative representatives of the evangelical movement.

Chapter Two

Political Liberalism in American Mainline and Catholic Churches

Although they are not this book's central concern, it is important to know something about the degree to which America's mainline Protestant denominations and segments of the American Catholic church have surrendered to various forms of left-wing thinking. The present-day referents of "mainline Protestantism" in the United States are the United Methodist Church, the Presbyterian Church, U.S.A., the Episcopal Church, the United Church of Christ, the Disciples of Christ, the Evangelical Lutheran Church in America, and the American Baptist Churches. While it is still possible to find biblically faithful churches and church leaders within these denominations, it is hardly realistic to deny that these organizations have grown increasingly more liberal theologically in our lifetime.[1]

Some in the evangelical Left view mainline liberals as allies and partners in their political ventures. This may explain why the evangelical Left is noticeably reluctant to criticize mainstream and Catholic liberals even when their theology deviates markedly from the more orthodox beliefs of the evangelicals.

THE RISE OF PROTESTANT MODERNISM

How did Protestant modernism, as it came to be called, come to differ from the earlier theological consensus of the larger American Protestant denominations. One author explains:

Liberalism not only tried to undermine faith in the cardinal doctrines of the church; it was also intensely humanistic in the sense that it believed man to be essentially good and fully able to solve his problems and build for himself a better world. The liberals were characterized by their great faith in human progress. They seemed to be incurably optimistic. Their theology gave the impression that God was present in the wonderful world of science and technology, working for the benefit of man. They emphasized the immanence of God, passing over His transcendence. They placed the religion of feeling above the authority of written revelation. They subjected the Bible to the judgment of reason in the way they applied historical and literary criticism to it, denying the possibility that God could reveal Himself in a supernatural way through the Scriptures. Thus the liberals sacrificed the Bible's authority on the altar of human reason.[2]

This radical revision of Christianity should have been given a new name, so different was it from the historic faith described in the Scriptures and explained in the church's ancient creeds.

While theological liberalism does not always beget political and economic liberalism, this has often been the case in the mainline churches. It is hardly surprising that, having abandoned the historic faith along with its promise of eternal life, many theologically liberal clergy sought fulfillment in a utopian vision of an exclusively earthly kingdom. Nor is it surprising that so many members of this early version of the Religious Left looked with favor on Soviet-style Marxism. Nobel laureate Friedrich Hayek was struck by the fascination liberal clergy have had for earthly utopias. He once suggested that since they had lost their faith in a supernatural revelation, the liberals probably "sought a refuge and consolation in a new 'social' religion which substitutes a temporal for a celestial promise of justice.... [they] hope that they can thus continue their striving to do good."[3]

K. L. Billingsley documents the shameful support that many socialist clergymen gave to Communist tyrants like Joseph Stalin and Mao Tse-tung.[4] Many left-wing American clergy acted as though Stalin was establishing the kingdom of God in the Soviet Union. Even while Stalin's secret police were murdering millions of their own countrymen, alleged spokesmen for Christ in America were praising what they saw as Stalin's efforts to bring about "a just social order." During the years of the Cold War, left-wing clergy in the mainline churches sometimes acted as if they wanted the Soviets and their allies to win. During the Vietnam War, many openly sided with the North Vietnamese cause. During the 1980s, Castro's Cuba and the Nicaraguan Sandinistas gave mainline liberals new causes to support.

CBS AND THE NATIONAL COUNCIL OF CHURCHES

In a 1978 article in *Harper's,* author Paul Seabury claimed that by the late 1960s, authorities in the Episcopal Church's national office "were dispensing millions of dollars of missionary funds collected from parishes and dioceses to radical political movements across the land—Black Power groups, migrant farm workers, Afro-American thespians, Puerto Rican nationalists, Marxist documentary film producers, and Third World liberation movements."[5] Seabury, a well-known political scientist and Episcopal layman, described how St. John the Divine, the great Episcopal cathedral in New York City, became a location for Sufi workshops in dervish dancing, ceremonies for Indians at Wounded Knee, Shinto ceremonies, Masses for the musical *Hair,* and radical political protest rallies. While Seabury's exposé was largely overlooked or ignored outside the inner circle of mainline hierarchies, it did serve as a stimulus for a significant airing of the issue on national television several years later.

The radically liberal nature of the mainline Protestant denominations and the National Council of Churches (NCC) first received national attention in a shocking segment of CBS Television's *60 Minutes* that aired on January 23, 1983. The program demonstrated NCC sympathy toward Marxist-Leninist revolutionaries and governments and documented the financial support the NCC and its member denominations have provided to such organizations. Of course, the money in question came from donations of faithful church members, many of whom probably had no intention of supporting terrorist groups or totalitarian states.

The furor over the *60 Minutes* broadcast lasted only a while. Americans tend to have short memories, and the only references to this program and the actions of NCC and mainline denominational officials it disclosed appear in books that, regrettably, few people have read. These works contain many astonishing revelations.

Rael Jean and Erich Isaac's *Coercive Utopians*

One of the more important of these books is *The Coercive Utopians*, written by Rael Jean Isaac and Erich Isaac. The groups and movements the authors discuss are "utopian" because "they assume that an ideal social order can be created in which man's potentialities can flower freely. They are "coercive" because in their zeal for attaining an ideal order they seek to impose their blueprints in ways that go beyond legitimate "persuasion."[6] The authors explain that the coercive utopians not only think a perfect society is possible, but they

> also believe that the society in which they live is deeply flawed, indeed hateful. And if one has to identify the single aspect of American life that they find most repugnant, it is our economic system. The reason for the abhorrence of capitalism varies among utopian groups. Churchmen, who have adopted a utopian perspective, believe that it fosters competition rather than the cooperation they define as a religious ideal.[7]

The United States, the Isaacs continue,

> is seen by many of the utopians as literally the worst society in the world. In so far as the utopians [had] real life models [in the 1980s when the Isaacs wrote], they are places like Cuba, Vietnam, Nicaragua, and China (at least until it moved toward the West). The glorification of socialized Third World

poverty reflects the romanticism of the utopians. Rural communal life, the outward show of worker participation in workplace assemblies, the rhetoric of egalitarianism, the block level of civil control which is seen as an expression of neighborhood solidarity and self-governance, the very absence of consumer goods, make these societies immensely appealing. That their chief distinguishing characteristic is the desire of vast numbers of their citizens to leave at almost any price does not daunt the utopians.[8]

The Isaacs describe how such opinions played out in the mainline churches as well as in various activist groups and liberal think tanks:

> Utopians dominate the leadership and professional staff of the mainline Protestant denominations and their related organizations, including the National Council of Churches. . . . They are the leaders of almost all the peace groups. . . . They are the intellectuals in a number of institutes and think tanks that have flourished in the soil of so-called "revisionist history," which places the blame for world tensions after World War II primarily on the United States.[9]

The Isaacs report how "The Great Episcopal cathedrals, St. John the Divine in New York City and Grace Cathedral in San Francisco, became centers of what Episcopal Canon William Rauscher has called 'the church in frenzy.'"[10] They document the massive financial support the hierarchy of the United Methodist Church provided for radical political groups.[11] Several of the groups supported by United Methodist funds were propagandists for such Communist states as Cuba and Vietnam.[12]

Various branches of the National Council of Churches, the Isaacs report, regularly attacked the United States as the source of all evil in the world. But if the United States was the NCC's negative ideal, what nations functioned as their positive ideal, as their model countries? "Astonishingly, these are Marxist Third World countries that have either severely restricted or all but eliminated religion."[13] The Isaacs document the Soviet Union's use of American mainline denominations as propaganda instruments.[14]

Paul Hollander's *Anti-Americanism*

In a book titled *Anti-Americanism*,[15] Paul Hollander, a professor of sociology at the University of Massachusetts, Amherst, provides numerous examples of what he regards as mainline malfeasance. He pays considerable attention to William Sloane Coffin, one-time chaplain at Yale University who then served as senior minister of the Riverside Church in New York City during much of the 1980s.

In the 1970s, Hollander states, Coffin served as an apologist for the Communist regime in North Vietnam. Coffin once claimed that "Communism is a page torn out of the Bible" and that "the social justice that's been achieved in ... North Vietnam [is] an achievement no Christian society on that scale has ever achieved."[16] When Coffin tired of defending Communist Vietnam, he threw his support behind the Marxist-Leninist Sandinista movement in Nicaragua. Riverside Church provided a public platform for such stars of the Sandinista movement as Daniel Ortega.

According to Hollander, Coffin illustrated an attitude common to both secular and religious leftists, namely, that the enemy of my enemy must be my friend. The enemy that is such a preoccupation of the American Left, of course, is the United States. This means, in Hollander's words, that "if the United States is hostile toward a country or political system, the latter must be doing something right and deserves support and sympathy. Thus the American attempts to overthrow or weaken the Sandinista regime almost automatically made it a recipient of the sympathy and solidarity of a full-time social critic of the United States, such as Coffin."[17]

Accompanying their hostility to the United States, Hollander adds, is the radicals' obsession with anti-anticommunism. Coffin's attitude, for example, "resembles those of the sympathizers with far-left movements or systems who nonetheless indignantly protest being labeled a Communist (or Marxist-Leninist) while being concurrently attracted to these ideas and their institutional or organizational embodiments."[18]

Turning to the World Council of Churches, Hollander states that it "has virtually institutionalized Western guilt toward the Third World, making it a cornerstone of its pronouncements and policies."[19] The NCC and WCC were notable for their refusal to criticize the Soviet Union, even for its invasion of Afghanistan. The concern of the NCC and WCC was directed instead toward efforts to demand that U.S. aid to anti-Soviet guerillas be ended.[20] Nor did the WCC criticize the Soviet Union for its denial of religious freedom to its citizens, even though it was quick to denounce similar evils in places like South Africa and Chile. Hollander's book cites numerous other examples of anti-Americanism and pro-Marxist actions on the part of religious leftists in the NCC and WCC.

K. L. Billingsley's *From the Mainline to the Sidelines*

Only political bias, poor judgment, or serious misinformation, K. L. Billingsley writes, "can account for the NCC's failure to see that Marxist-Leninist regimes persecute Christians for their faith" and "seek to eradicate all religious belief."[21] NCC officials have visited such states as Cuba, often without making any effort to help oppressed Christian brothers and sisters. Even worse is the fact that the NCC "has on occasion applauded the tormentors for 'fulfilling' the Gospel—which is a little like cheering for the lions at the Roman Coliseum."[22] Especially telling, Billingsley thinks, was the NCC's silence about the attack on Afghanistan by Russian troops on December 25, 1979. During the ten years of the Russian occupation, more than one million people were killed in Afghanistan, while another four million fled into exile. Yet, the NCC mever made a single public announcement about the Soviet occupation.

THE CATHOLIC CHURCH IN THE UNITED STATES

American Roman Catholics have traditionally been politically and culturally conservative. But during the last three decades, American Catholicism has undergone significant theological changes. Theologically conservative Protestants and Catholics used to share a common worldview that saw the world as the creation of an almighty God who has the power and the will to act supernaturally within his creation. Roman Catholics and evangelicals used to share a belief in the Virgin Birth, the resurrection of Christ, and the final judgment that would separate humans into saved and lost. But this has changed for many as large numbers of Catholic academicians, priests, and nuns have adopted various elements of Protestant liberal theology.[23] This has led many Catholic thinkers to adopt a hostile biblical criticism that has compromised the inspiration and authority of Scripture along with an antisupernaturalism that rejects the essential miracles of the Christian faith. This loss of faith is now apparent on the campuses of many of the best-known Catholic universities.

American Catholicism has also changed politically since 1960. Conservative Catholics ranked among this country's strongest opponents of communism. They were thoughtful enemies of secularism, humanism, and the liberal welfare state.[24] When pollsters began to test public opinion on the abortion issue in the early sixties, Roman Catholic opposition was far greater than that found among Protestants.[25]

Since then, large cracks have appeared in the political and social thinking of many educated Catholics as various ideologies such as neo-Marxism, the New Left, and democratic socialism began to have a greater impact. The 1985 Pastoral Letter on the American economy published by the American Catholic bishops was one indication of how things were going within the hierarchy of the American Catholic church. The bishops' letter was essentially a neo-Marxist critique of capitalism coupled with a plea for an expansion of the liberal welfare state and continued redistribution of wealth. Many Protestant members of the Religious Left, including the evangelicals who will be studied later in this book, welcomed that document. Its leftist ideology resonated with their own redistributionist sentiments.[26]

Symptomatic of the radicalism of some in the American Catholic hierarchy was Raymond G. Hunthausen, Archbishop of Seattle, who once called an American nuclear submarine "the Auschwitz of Puget Sound."[27] Growing Catholic support for more hard-core Marxist views became apparent in the support these radicals gave to the Sandinista movement in Nicaragua. It was also apparent in the unexpectedly rapid spread of liberation theology within important segments of Catholic (and Protestant) thinking.

Put in the simplest possible terms, liberation theology is a movement that downplays the historic, doctrinal side of Christianity and emphasizes instead the importance of Christian action on behalf of poor and oppressed people.[28] Liberation theology can appear attractive to dedicated Christians, who find it easy to identify with the underdogs of the world. And what group of underdogs deserves compassion and help more than the poor and oppressed? It is worth noting that liberation theologians seemed to care only about those poor and oppressed people who did not happen to be oppressed by Marxist regimes. They never talked, for example, about poor and oppressed peoples in the Central and Eastern European nations under the thumb of Communist governments.

One thing that Catholic liberationists tried to cover over was their propensity for theological heresy. Some were condemned by the Vatican for denying the Christian church's historic understanding of such essential beliefs as the Atonement, the Trinity, the deity of Jesus Christ, and his bodily resurrection from the dead.[29]

The Case of the Maryknoll Order

A striking example of a Roman Catholic order that lost its bearings is the Catholic Foreign Mission Society of America, often referred to as the Maryknoll order because its headquarters are located in Maryknoll, New York. Richard John Neuhaus sets the stage: "The Maryknollers were established many years ago to win the world to Christ and his Church. Many remember Maryknollers chiefly for their heroic mission work in China."[30] But things changed dramatically. As liberal theology took over, the Maryknollers became practitioners of what is politely called religious pluralism.[31] Neuhaus observes,

> Aficionados of irony will appreciate that years later, during the rule of Chairman Mao, the Maryknollers would be promoting the view that China was the most Christian nation in the world, albeit without Christ and his Church. Carrying Karl Rahner's notion of 'anonymous Christians' to an extreme, it is the triumph of the missionary enterprise by fiat. Certainly it is much more convenient than the heroic but apparently misguided course of Maryknollers of old who gave their lives to winning unbelievers for the Gospel one by one.[32]

Paul Hollander observes that Maryknoll missionaries who were supportive of left-wing governments in Central America and who opposed American support for anti-Communist guerillas had profound influence on then-Speaker of the House Thomas (Tip) O'Neill.[33] Left-wing church activists seem clearly to have played a role in influencing Congress to reject President Ronald Reagan's request for military aid to support the Nicaraguan contras.

Supporters of liberation theology want people to overlook the heavy Marxist presence in their system. They want people to think that liberation theology is simply a product of conscientious and compassionate Christians' demonstrating their love and concern for the poor and oppressed. In truth, however, liberationists have appeared to care only about the poor and oppressed people who interested them. Liberationist efforts to address the issue of poverty typically did so from an unabashed Marxist perspective.

What finally produced the collapse of liberation thought outside the United States and Western Europe was the set of incredible events that some now call "the revolutions of 1989." The sudden, sweeping changes that affected Eastern Europe and that eventually stabbed deeply into the heart of the former Soviet Union have unveiled once and for all what many economists and social theorists have argued for years: the bankruptcy of socialism.

It helped neither the reputation nor the morale of the advocates of liberation theology that the revolutions of 1989 and the new Russian revolution of 1991 repudiated the very ideas they held so dear. Many better-known Latin American liberationists have since distanced themselves from their former beliefs and embraced, however tentatively, an idea once deemed unthinkable: that capitalism just might have something to offer the world's poor after all.

North American liberationists, however, have been more intractable in their fanatical attachment to socialism. Those who dominate the mainline Protestant denominations and their left-wing allies within American Roman Catholicism are not especially happy these days. They and their institutions may well be the last vestiges of the now discredited version of liberation theology. Their type of liberation theology supported means that were counterproductive because they impeded genuine and lasting progress toward the desired goal of real liberation. Liberation theologians understood little of how the poor may be delivered from economic oppression, opting only for repeatedly smaller pieces of an economic pie that, they insisted, could never grow larger. They were disturbingly complacent about democracy and noticeably lax about how the Christian faith deals with the most important kind of liberation—liberation from sin.[34]

THE "WHY?" QUESTION

Why have so many clergymen, college and seminary professors, and denominational leaders been controlled by leftist ideology? Paul Hollander explains this in terms of their eager surrender to what he calls the ideology of the "adversary culture," about which I will say more in the next chapter. This radical ideology has for the last quarter-century thrived in academic settings. But why, Hollander asks, has this package of attitudes and beliefs been so influential over clergy who are not part of an academic environment?

According to Hollander, "Many of them are doubtless influenced by the messages emanating from higher levels of church hierarchy: the NCC, the Catholic bishops; they are also bound to reflect in some measure the teachings they were exposed to at their seminaries in the course of their training."[35] Part of the answer, he suggests, may also be a confused identification with people they regard as the world's underdogs. At best, however, these observations seem to be only part of the reason. We are not looking at people known for their political moderation. Why are so many leaders of American churches supportive of revolutionary groups?

Rael Jean and Erich Isaac put the question another way: "Why is this [church] leadership so critical of United States' economic, social and political institutions? Why are Marxist regimes, although they violate human rights far more massively than the governments these churchmen attack [especially the United States], exempt from criticism? Why, on the contrary, are such regimes praised, and their support groups given financial aid? Why should Marxism exert any attraction at all for churchmen when the antipathy of Marxism to religion is one of its best-known characteristics?"[36]

The Isaacs identify ignorance, romanticism, bureaucratic isolation, and naïveté as important parts of the answer. But there must be more. "While the dislike of capitalism and the attraction of Marxism is old," they write, "the hatred of the United States is new. While the yearning for major social transformation is old, the acceptance by churchmen of the idea of violence is new."[37] This hostility and hatred toward the United States and this romantic attachment to revolutionary violence are phenomena that we will have to examine more fully in the next chapter.

But still another question must be answered. The religious leftists' alternative is a utopian illusion, a God who has failed. What kind of person, K. L. Billingsley asks, is "continually drawn to phantom kingdoms of heaven on earth, even to ones that persecute Christians? Why, when they are often such smart and caring people, do they employ their faculties in defense of a system founded on coercion?"[38] Billingsley's answers are especially relevant for members of the evangelical Left.

First, "Since the Bible does command care for the poor, there is a sharing of rhetoric. Revolutionaries say they are concerned for the poor. Radical Christians believe them. Unfortunately, it is often forgotten that once the poor and humble and meek are exalted, they too become the high and mighty, themselves fit to be put down."[39]

Second, Billingsley also thinks an irrational reaction against childhood fundamentalisms that exalted God and country may be at work in some cases. In such instances, radicals jump from one simplistic worldview to a second. The political fundamentalism they substitute for the religious fundamentalism of their childhood requires a similar leap of faith, a similar suspension of their critical faculties, and a similar commitment of their whole being. In Billingsley's opinion,

> [T]here is a death wish at work in the world and . . . this is part of it. How else can one explain Christians admiring a system that would make them unnecessary? There is nothing rational about it. Yet many in the West, not just radical Christians, tend to sympathize with developments that would mean the end of their societies, their religions, themselves, and the rest of us with them. They blow the trumpet that brings their own walls tumbling down. This is how civilizations end. Not with a bang or even a whimper, but with a death wish.[40]

Third, there is a very simple reason, Billingsley suggests, why people believe lies. It is not because the lies are plausible, but because the people want desperately to believe the lies.

> How else can one explain religious writers, clergy, activists, and college professors who are determined, come what may, to believe discarded dogmas, to overlook any brutality, to accept any explanation as long as it comes from the proper comandante. They want to preserve intact the hope that some of the most militant and obscurantist tyrannies ever to exist on earth can be relied upon to champion peace, Christian social action, the elimination of poverty, the brotherhood of man, and all the good causes to which they

have dedicated their lives. They believe this, not because of any evidence, but because they want to.[41]

Fourth, Billingsley explains why he and so many others view the behavior of the radical Religious Left as an exercise in madness: "The Christian faith is being turned by some into a public relations apparatus for totalitarianism."[42] There are and have been many mysteries in the Christian faith, but perhaps none so challenging as figuring out what has gone on in the thinking of Religious Left extremists.

CONCLUSION

I plan to say little more about mainline Protestant and Roman Catholic purveyors of the Religious Left in the rest of this book. Naturally, they will be mentioned here and there, as they must. But for the most part, the remainder of the book will focus on another manifestation of the spirit of the Religious Left—namely, the one led by a group of individuals who profess a commitment to a theologically conservative understanding of the Christian faith.

When these people first began to be noticed in the late sixties and early seventies, they were quite proud of their distinctive place within political liberalism. While political liberalism had typically been the preferred position of theologically liberal Christians, the members of what came to be known as the evangelical Left professed a commitment to the beliefs and practices of American evangelicalism. That is, they claimed to accept the doctrines of traditional Christian orthodoxy, they often professed a high view of Scripture,[43] and they believed in the importance of evangelism and personal conversion. In other words, these political liberals were theologically conservative Protestants, more or less.[44]

It is this variety of the Religious Left that is the major focus of this book. The question of why I have decided to concentrate on this specific collection of people is certainly appropriate.

My answer is a simple one: I am an evangelical Christian writing this book for an audience that, I expect, will be composed largely of evangelicals. My publisher is one of the better-known evangelical publishing houses in the United States. Both my publisher and I hope that large numbers of people who may not consider themselves evangelicals will read this book and profit from it. Protestant liberals in the mainline churches, conservative and liberal Roman Catholics, and secularists in higher education, government, and the media together make up just a small part of the larger audience we envision. Moreover, because the problems of the American church are duplicated elsewhere throughout the world, I believe that international readers will also benefit from much that I discuss.

Chapter Three

The Adversary Generation

This is the first of two chapters that explore the underlying network of ideas and movements necessary to any adequate understanding of today's leaders of the evangelical Left. These people did not become leftists overnight; they have been shaped, to a great extent, by their responses to what has happened in America in the last quarter-century.

The dominant theme in these two chapters is Marxism. As I explain in chapter 4, the word "Marxism" has assumed several meanings over the years. It is important to recognize that one can be justly termed a Marxist without implying a commitment to Marxist-Leninist totalitarianism.

THE NEW LEFT

The term "New Left" refers to the trendy radicalism that many college students and college dropouts found exhilarating in the late sixties. During the ten years of its organized existence, the New Left changed dramatically. It mutated from a leftist-idealist student movement into a band of crypto-Communist nihilists.

The New Left was Jim Wallis's political and ideological home during the late sixties, and he has never really abandoned his New Left anti-Americanism. What did change was his discovery that he could continue to be anti-American while putting a religious veneer on his radical politics.

It is important to distinguish the New Left from the familiar type of liberalism that dominated the Democratic party through the election of 1968 and that largely controlled the Republican party until the election of Ronald Reagan in 1980. The liberalism of the two major parties that supported the transfer of increasing amounts of political power to the central government differed only in the preferred pace for this transfer. The liberals' solution to any kind of problem was to let the Congress pass legislation empowering the creation of a new branch of the federal bureaucracy. This was then followed by a flood of new laws and regulations along with an increase in taxes to pay for the whole thing. Then everyone sat back and watched things get worse. They also watched the federal government grow in size and power. This has been the Washington way—the liberal way—of doing business.[1]

What came to be called the Old Left was a liberalism drunk with the wine of socialist (or at least some kind of) Marxist doctrine. When the New Left came along, it condemned the Old Left as insufficiently revolutionary. One way to see the major differences between the Old and New Left is the following chart:[2]

Old Left	New Left
1. Forms alliances with liberals	1. Views liberals as the enemy
2. Workers are the revolutionary class	2. Intellectuals are the revolutionary class
3. Workers are exploited	3. Workers are alienated
4. Industrial socialism	4. Post-industrial socialism
5. Gradualism	5. Revolutionary change
6. Central planning and control	6. Decentralized decisions
7. Liberals want to free others	7. Radicals want to free themselves
8. Soviet distortion of Marx	8. Discovery of the real Marx (Marcuse)
9. Realism	9. Utopianism
10. Serves the people	10. Serves to live authentically
11. Work is necessary (always conflict)	11. Work can be abolished (no conflict)

12. Intellectual	12. Anti-intellectual and anti-theoretical
13. Ideology	13. Style
14. Vanguardist and elitist	14. Populist
15. State capitalism (socialism)	15. Anarcho-socialism

All of these points except 4 and 11 require some commentary.

1. The Old Left found it convenient to work with mainstream American liberals—at least until the situation was ripe—for more significant change and the election of their own people to positions of power. The New Left hated liberals and viewed them as the enemy.[3] Of course, New Left radicals also despised members of the Old Left.

2. In traditional Marxist fashion, the Old Left looked upon the working class with the same fervent hope that Marx and Engels expressed in the closing line of the *Communist Manifesto:* "Workers of the world, unite!" The New Left sensed that the workers were a lost cause, hopelessly seduced by capitalism. The new and the true revolutionary class was composed of intellectuals— namely, college students and professors like them. Their Marxist manifesto was the writings of philosopher Herbert Marcuse, who taught at the University of California at San Diego.

3. The Old Left followed classic Marxist dogma that the workers were exploited, but the New Left had learned from Marcuse that the real problem of the workers was that they suffered from alienation.

5. The Old Left represented the position known as democratic socialism. They were repelled by Lenin's emphasis on violent revolution. They were proponents of peaceful socialism, slowly put into place over years of legislative activity by increasingly liberal government leaders. The New Left longed for revolution and sought to produce it.

6. The Old Left reflected a commitment to big government, in which all planning and control came from the central authority. The New Left, at least early on, used rhetoric supportive of decentralized decision making.[4] Of course, this proved to be one

of the movement's weak points, since it eventually led to splitting into numerous competing groups.

7. The inspiration of the Old Left was its obsession with "freeing others." The radicals were embarked on a journey of self-discovery. Their obsession was to free themselves from whatever chains they believed bound them.

8. The Old Left condemned Lenin, Stalin, and the Soviet system for distorting Marxism. The New Left supposedly found Marx's "true" meaning in some unpublished ramblings he wrote in 1843–44. This hidden legacy found expression in the writings of Marcuse, whom the New Left honored as the discoverer of the true Marx.

9. The Old Left was realistic in the sense that it wanted programs and policies that would work and help repair the real world. The New Left was utterly utopian; the last thing on any of their minds was realism.

10. The Old Left viewed themselves as people committed to serving others. The New Left's commitment was to live the kinds of "authentic" lives they found described in the writings of thinkers like Jean Paul Sartre.

12. The Old Left was intellectual—that is, it thought that mind and ideas could triumph over society's ills. The New Left was rabidly anti-intellectual; it was opposed to theory.

13. The Old Left had an ideology. All the New Left had was a certain style.

14. The Old Left saw themselves as elitists, as the vanguard of the future. The New Left were populists, suspicious of any concentration of power in a few people.

15. The ultimate objective of the Old Left was state capitalism, that is, heavy centralized government control over a severely hampered market economy. The New Left was anarchistic in the sense of rejecting a role for government in the economy of the nation. Such actions as general strikes and even sabotage would serve to bring industry and government under the control of labor unions.

The early members of the New Left were obsessed with what they saw as America's sickening materialism and the hollowness of the American dream. Government and the economy, they argued, needed to be responsive to popular control. They condemned Cold War policies as bankrupt. They rejected past liberal and socialist teachings as inadequate for a wealthy, modern, technological society. They saw the potential of the university as a radical center for changing America.

At first the New Left was a movement intent upon imposing its own vision of participatory democracy on America. Its people were active in the civil rights movement. But the Vietnam War caused widespread disaffection with America as well as with the ideals of the New Left's early phase. This disaffection led to a loss of love of country. The new New Left, in effect, declared war on America. According to Peter Collier and David Horowitz,

> Sympathy for America's alleged victims developed into an identification with America's real enemies. In 1968, the Students for a Democratic Society (SDS)—the heart of the New Left—converted to "Marxism-Leninism," and the following year its convention broke into hostile rival factions, chanting the names of Chairman Mao and "Uncle" Ho [Chi Minh]. In a few short years, the Communist dictators of China and North Vietnam had become the household gods of the New Left.[5]

Collier and Horowitz, both hard-core New Leftists in their younger days, described some of the steps that led to their rejection of their old radicalism.

> In the years after America's defeat in Vietnam, we were presented with a balance sheet showing the sobering consequences of our politics. New Left orthodoxy had scorned the idea that the war was about North Vietnamese aggression and Soviet expansion, but soon after the American pullout, North Vietnamese armies were in Cambodia and Laos, and the Russians were occupying the bases at Cam Ranh Bay and Da Nang and securing exploration rights to natural resources in Indochina in unmistakably imperial style. What we had dismissed as impossible was happening with dizzying speed. Far from being liberated, South Vietnam was now

occupied by a conquering army from the North. The "blood-bath" our opponents predicted took place in the form of tens of thousands of summary executions, while many of the "indigenous" revolutionaries of the NLF [National Liberation Front], whom we had supported, disappeared into "reeduca-tion" camps or joined the "boat people" exodus to freedom in the West. In Cambodia, two million peasants died at the hands of the Communist Khmer Rouge, protégés of Hanoi and beneficiaries of the New Left's 'solidarity' with the revo-lutionary cause. It was a daunting lesson: more people had been killed in the first two years of the Communist peace than in the thirteen years of America's war.[6]

Following the American withdrawal from Vietnam, the Soviet Union then demonstrated how totalitarianism abhors a vacuum by expanding its influence into Africa, Central America, Southeast Asia, and in the most brutal of ways, Afghanistan.

THE ADVERSARY CULTURE

Many people think that little survives from the radical Left's rejec-tion of American society during the 1960s and 1970s. Paul Hol-lander disagrees.[7] It is true, he admits, that many of the older radical movements and organizations seemed to have disappeared for several years. But although they were publicly less visible, they continued to survive and grow below the surface. By the late 1980s the adversary culture (Hollander's term for the radical Left) had resurfaced with a vengeance.

While in its earlier incarnations the adversary culture was part of the counterculture, many of its beliefs, values, and atti-tudes have become part of mainstream America. During the 1968 Democratic convention, the representatives of the adversary cul-ture were outside the convention, rioting in the streets. During the 1988 and 1992 Democratic conventions, they were inside helping to run the show. In the mid-1990s some of them could be found in the Congress, in the federal bureaucracies, and in the

Clinton Administration. Some of them—like Jim Wallis—can also be found in the evangelical Left.

Without question, Hollander points out, the place where this radicalism is most evident is the college campus, where large numbers of faculty engage in politicizing their disciplines and their institutions. The college campus is one place where the dispositions of the old adversary culture (the mindset of the radicals of the 1960s and 1970s) still thrive. Vestiges of the adversary culture are still evident in the statements and actions of the liberals who control the hierarchies of America's mainline Protestant denominations. Surprisingly, they are found also on the campuses of numerous evangelical colleges and seminaries.

According to reliable sources, some ten thousand American college and university professors freely identify themselves as Marxists. To this number can be added thousands of others who strongly sympathize with left-wing political and social values. Paul Hollander writes, "Even if the majority of the students in the nation today do not subscribe to [this] mentality, large and vocal portions of their teachers do, especially in the humanities and social sciences. My own discipline, sociology, has, for example been quite thoroughly politicized and probably a majority of its practitioners take [this way of thinking] for granted."[8] This army of radical professors has more than a dozen Marxist journals at its disposal, which it uses to repeat familiar diatribes against America, capitalism, economic freedom, and whatever else the Left happens to despise at the moment.

We must never forget how, in 1989, enslaved peoples in many Marxist states around the world rebelled against tyranny and brought about, among other things, the destruction of the Berlin Wall. A special irony in this did not escape the notice of nationally syndicated columnist Georgie Anne Geyer: "When American students return to U.S. colleges and universities, they will make an extraordinary voyage—from a summer where the whole world was denouncing and renouncing Marxism to just about the only place where self-righteous Marxists still exist and thrive."[9]

While the nations of Eastern Europe were denouncing—indeed, overthrowing—Marxism, the doctrine still flourished in

American schools, "where Marxist academics do not deign to take notice of the real world." Geyer quotes Arnold Beichman of the Hoover Institute: "The Marxist academics are today's power elite in the universities and [because of] the magic of the tenure system they have become self-perpetuating. . . . It has successfully substituted Marxist social change as the goal of learning, instead of a search for objective truth."[10]

In spite of this dramatic reversal of political fortunes, Geyer continues, "[U]topian Marxist thinking is infecting American education on virtually every level." She finds the explanation for this "in the rarefied utopianism of so many American academics." This Marxism neutralizes "the legitimacy, the genuine intellectuality, and the mission of America and its newest generation."

We dare not misunderstand, Geyer warns. These Marxists are not interested in an education that opens the American mind or heart. Their objective is to subvert the truth in an effort to capture the minds and hearts of students for their radical cause. "While Eastern Europeans are finally freeing themselves from horrendous falsehoods, such as the Russian denial of the Stalin-Hitler pact that divided up Eastern Europe, most of our unhampered, pampered professors are avidly embracing that pact's philosophy." In Geyer's words, these men and women "are intellectual disgraces to a free society."

NICARAGUA AND THE SANDINISTAS

With the Sandinista party playing a prominent but by no means exclusive role, the people of Nicaragua overthrew the hated dictator Anastasio Somoza in July 1979. Quickly breaking their promise to support democracy, the Sandinistas consolidated their control of the country and began marching Nicaragua down the road to Marxism.[11] K. L. Billingsley explains, "Once in power the Sandinistas made short shrift of democratic pretense—U.S. benevolence and their own pledges to the OAS [Organization of American States] notwithstanding—and installed a Marxist-Leninist regime that reflected the Cuban model. The United States continued to give aid to Nicaragua, $120,000,000 and 100,000 tons of food from 1979–1981."[12]

The evangelical Left and others frequently denied the Leninist commitments of the Sandinistas. It is difficult to guess how many of them actually believed this or simply used the claim to cover their real support for a hard-core Marxist-Leninist revolution. But Sandinista support for Marxism-Leninism was obvious to anyone interested in finding it. Humberto Ortega, the defense minister and the brother of Daniel Ortega, the Nicaraguan president at the time, stated that "our doctrine is Marxism-Leninism."[13] After the death of the Soviet leader Konstantin Chernenko in 1985, the Nicaraguan leaders praised the Soviet leader as a "great statesman and untiring fighter for the cause of world peace and solidarity."[14] They declared a period of mourning for Chernenko.

Almost from the time they gained control of Nicaragua, the Sandinistas made clear their support for Cuba and the Soviet Union. They signed an accord with the Communist party of the U.S.S.R. and publicly supported the Soviet invasion of Afghanistan. They helped to spread violence to other nations by supporting Marxist insurgencies. They indicated their hostility to the United States by referring to "the Yankee enemy of mankind" in the lyrics of the national anthem. They also boasted that "over here, over there, the Yankees will die everywhere."[15]

Collier and Horowitz have published an account of Fidel Castro's role in the Sandinista takeover of Nicaragua. There is no question that the support given the Sandinistas by American radicals was a major reason for their partial success in maintaining control in the face of major opposition from Nicaraguan supporters of democracy.[16] Collier and Horowitz also discuss Castro's role in unifying the Marxist guerillas in El Salvador and the role the Sandinistas played in supplying them with weapons.[17]

Ernesto Cardenal, a radical Catholic priest who was eventually disciplined by the Pope, was the Sandinistas' minister of culture. He believed that "Marxism is the only solution for the world. For me the revolution and the Kingdom of heaven, mentioned in the Gospels, are the same thing. A Christian should embrace

Marxism if he wants to be with God and with men.... As Mankind matures, religion will start disappearing slowly until it vanishes completely."[18]

This shocking subordination of religious belief to a political agenda by a priest, no less, is echoed by Maryknoll priest Miguel D'Escoto, the Sandinistas' foreign minister. In 1987 D'Escoto was awarded the Lenin Peace Prize by the Communist party of the U.S.S.R. In accepting the award, he revealed more than he should have about his support for Marxism-Leninism:

> This prize makes us Nicaraguans come into even closer contact with Lenin, that great personality of your state and of all mankind who is the passionate champion of peace.... I believe the Soviet Union is a great torch which emits hope for the preservation of peace on our planet. Always in the vanguard of the overall struggle for peace, the Soviet Union has become the personification of ethical and moral norms in international relations. I admire the revolutionary principles and consistency of the foreign policy of the Communist Party of the fraternal Soviet Union.[19]

A favorite activity for American leftists during the 1980s was arranging political pilgrimages to Nicaragua. Between 1979 and 1987, it is reported, some 40,000 Americans traveled to Nicaragua on such pilgrimages. Many of the American pilgrims to Nicaragua were students at Christian colleges and seminaries who were led there by left-wing faculty at their institutions.[20]

The central attraction for many of these political tourists was what Tom Carson, writing sympathetically in *Village Voice*, called "A renewal of belief in the possibility of revolution."[21] Paul Hollander explains, "Most visitors went to Nicaragua in search of vindication of their critiques of the American political and social system— a desire which, as had been the case before, was combined with the hope of finding a new and authentic expression of socialist values, free of the taints and errors of other similar systems."[22]

Various spokesmen for the American radical Left explain the allure and excitement that Nicaragua held for them. According to

Martin Peretz, "Nicaragua remains the revolutionary idyll, filling the vast emotional void created by the sequential disenchantments with the Soviet Union ... China ... Cuba and ... Vietnam."[23] The radical magazine *Mother Jones* stated that "Backwater Nicaragua was the world center of the New Left.... Fantasy was realism in Nicaragua.... everyone who went through our own North American New Left, or who identifies with it after the fact, finds the Sandinistas so appealing.... it's so natural for us to look at them and explain, 'Hey, those are our guys down there.' ... we feel a natural solidarity."[24]

Few Sandinista leaders were Christians in any traditional sense of the word. Under different circumstances the Sandinistas might have treated the Nicaraguan church as Castro persecuted the church in Cuba. But the situation in Nicaragua differed enough to require other tactics. One reason was the strong religious faith of the Nicaraguan people.

Peasants and workers with strong religious convictions have often been the strongest opponents of communism. This was certainly true in Poland and was likely to be true in Nicaragua, two of the most heavily Roman Catholic nations in the world. Liberation theology afforded the hard-line Leninists in the Sandinista party a way to defuse religious opposition to Marxism in Nicaragua. If Catholic peasants could be persuaded that Marxist values were Christian values, their initial resistance could be weakened significantly. What made the Sandinistas' tactic even more promising was having their own radicalized priests or pastors teach the peasants the "Christian" version of Marx. After the peasants' initial opposition to Marxism wore down, efforts could be made to win the new Marxist "Christians" to the more radical views of Marxism-Leninism, the real but cleverly disguised ideology of the Sandinistas.

In other words, the Sandinistas used liberation theology as an anesthetic while they removed the patient's Christianity. Liberation theology became the Trojan horse by which Marxism-Leninism gained access to nations like Nicaragua that otherwise would have rejected it on religious grounds. Even liberationist José

Míguez Bonino acknowleged the extent to which liberation theology could help overcome religious opposition to communism.[25]

The attention the Sandinistas paid to Christianity did not involve any change in their Marxist philosophy or, for that matter, an openness or new tolerance toward religion. It simply meant a new consciousness of the need to *use* Christians and, as a corollary, a tactical decision not to present an openly anti-religious face. Professed Nicaraguan Christians who supported the revolution encouraged other Christians to work with the Sandinista government. They did this by reinterpreting Christian beliefs to endorse the main Marxist-Leninist tenets regarding man and society. They claimed that true Christianity is, in fact, Marxism.[26]

Cooperation between Christians and Marxists in Nicaragua under Sandinista rule led many Christians to abandon their religious faith and convert to atheistic communism.[27] Christian supporters of the Nicaraguan revolution lent credibility to the Sandinistas' contention that they were not Marxist-Leninists but a novel regime in which Christianity and revolution could walk together. In truth, these "revolutionary Christians" became a visible front to attack the Christian churches of Nicaragua and to undermine their authority and teachings, thus minimizing for the Sandinistas the potentially high cost of a more direct confrontation with the Catholic church.

Ironically, the revolutionary Christians also helped hide from the view of Christians abroad the fact that there was religious persecution in Nicaragua throughout the years of Sandinista rule.[28] While liberation theology in Nicaragua originally inspired Christians to oppose a right-wing dictatorship, it later became a tool to justify support for a left-wing dictatorship.

But then the Sandanistas were defeated in the election of early 1990. It is difficult to find words to describe their actions during the two months between their electoral defeat and Violeta Chamorro's inauguration as Nicaragua's democratically elected president. Under the headline "The Sandinistas' Greedy Goodbye," *Time* magazine described the "shameless pillaging" of the country, in which the Sandinistas stole as much as $700 million worth of booty, including $24 million from Nicaragua's Central Bank.[29] Former president Daniel Ortega now lives in a confiscated house valued at $950,000. Miguel D'Escoto, the priest who was the Sandinistas' foreign minister, owns one of the more expensive mansions in Managua, acquired for a mere $13,000. Others near the top of the Sandinista hierarchy profited as well. The Sandinistas gave none of this $700 million of land, property, and cash to ease the poverty and misery of Nicaragua's poor. Tom Sine, once a fervent admirer and supporter of the Sandinistas, is one of the few evangelical liberals to criticize them:

> During the eighties, the Sandinistas righteously promoted their revolution in Nicaragua as a movement for the poor. They forcefully denounced the rich and powerful as the source of all evil.... Today, however, many of the Sandinista leaders show signs of having succumbed to the greed they once denounced. Some have become both wealthy and preoccupied with protecting their wealth in ways that directly contradict the principles of their revolution.[30]

The Sandinistas proved what really lies beyond Marxist's revolutionary rhetoric: the accumulation of power and wealth.

As a surprising footnote to all this, K. L. Billingsley notes that

> *His,* the magazine of Inter-Varsity Christian Fellowship, devoted eight pages, a full 25 percent of a thirty-two page issue (January, 1984) to what amounted to a free political advertisement for the [then Marxist] Nicaraguan government. Junta members, including Daniel Ortega (appropriately shown in military uniform), were given carte blanche to express their views with only the mildest criticism of their policies allowed. In addition, *His* advertised a Nicaraguan information packet, decidedly slanted in the direction of the junta. *His* had never done anything remotely approaching this before.[31]

One can encounter many surprises when exploring the terrain of the evangelical Left.

Chapter Four

Of Marx and Men

It makes no sense to pretend that Marxist theories have no relevance to the kinds of liberalism in view in this book. Liberals resent the subject of Marxism being raised because of its potential for negative public relations. When the evangelical Left gets together—and I have been present on a number of such occasions—only a totally uninformed person could fail to sense the Marxian theories floating through the air.

THE RELIGIOUS LEFT'S ATTACK ON CAPITALISM

Paul Hollander points out that socialism has definite snob appeal among the intellectual elite. It is chic to be a socialist.

> The appeals and values associated with socialism ... have provided the most powerful incentive for the suspension of critical thinking among large contingents of Western intellectuals.... The word "socialism" has retained, despite all historical disappointments associated with regimes calling themselves socialist, a certain magic which rarely fails to disarm or charm these intellectuals and which inspires renewed hope that its most recent incarnation will be *the* authentic one, or at least more authentic than previous ones have been.[1]

> Needless to say, Hollander continues, "There is little evidence that intellectuals, or for that matter nonintellectuals, living in countries considered socialist are similarly charmed or disarmed by the idea of socialism."[2]

The writings of the Religious Left typically exhibit adulation for socialism and contempt for capitalism. A prime example of this hostility toward capitalism can be found in the book *Christians and Marxists* by José Míguez Bonino, a Latin American Protestant. Míguez Bonino first delivered the content of his book to evangelical audiences in London, England, under the auspices of John Stott, noted British evangelical and former rector of All Souls Church in London. The book, published by a noted evangelical publishing house, has been widely used as a required textbook in evangelical colleges and seminaries.

According to Míguez Bonino, "[T]he basic ethos of capitalism is definitely anti-Christian: it is the maximizing of economic gain, the raising of man's grasping impulse, the idolising of the strong, the subordination of man to the economic production.... In terms of their basic ethos, Christians must criticise capitalism radically, in its fundamental intention."[3] Míguez Bonino's book discusses Communists like Lenin, Mao Tse-tung, and Fidel Castro in the same reverent tones he uses to describe Christian saints and martyrs. Míguez Bonino reports how he is moved by "their deep compassion for human suffering and their fierce hatred of oppression and exploitation," neglecting to mention the millions who were oppressed, exploited, and murdered at their command.[4]

In one of his more surprising claims, Míguez Bonino writes, "Indeed, when we observe the process of building a socialist society in China ... we see a significant, even preponderant, importance given to the creation of a new man, a solidary human being who places the common good before his own individual interest."[5] Yet the China that Míguez Bonino thought so highly of was the China of Mao Tse-tung, which the Chinese themselves have since denounced. Sociologist Peter Berger provides a healthy antidote to Míguez Bonino's ethical short-sightedness when he writes, "*Even if* it were true that Maoism had vanquished hunger among China's poor, this achievement could not morally justify the horrors inflicted by the regime—horrors that entailed the killing of millions of human beings and the imposition of a merciless totalitarian rule on the survivors."[6]

But Míguez Bonino is not through praising Marxist dictator-ships. He writes:

> The political and economic quality and the human value of socialist revolutions has consistently increased as we move from the USSR to China and Cuba. The social cost has been reduced, the measure of compulsion and repression, partic-ularly in the last case, has been minimised, the welfare of the people has been given at least as much priority as eco-nomic development, the disruptive consequences of a blind drive towards industrialization have been avoided. The Chi-nese and Cuban revolutions have created a sense of partici-pation and achievement on the part of the people and have stimulated a feeling of dignity and moral determination.[7]

It is troubling to see how ideology has blinded Míguez Bonino to the horrible human cost of the regimes he admires so deeply. Such words would not be surprising if uttered by a paid propa-gandist of Mao or Castro, but they come from a self-professed evangelical who was speaking and writing to other evangelicals. One must wonder why Míguez Bonino was so silent about the mil-lions who died under Communist rule in China, the U.S.S.R., and Cambodia. Why did he fail to mention the persecution of the Christian church (and other religions) by the dictators he finds so admirable?

Another book widely hailed by the evangelical Left is *The Good News of the Kingdom Coming* by Andrew Kirk. Kirk was associate director of the London Institute for Contemporary Christianity, the group that gave Míguez Bonino the platform for the lectures on which his book is based. The institute had strong ties both to John Stott and to All Souls Church. Kirk's book, from a different evangelical publisher, also received wide use as a text-book in evangelical schools.

Like Míguez Bonino, Kirk holds that capitalism is incompat-ible with biblical principles.[8] He contends that the traditional evangelical definition of the gospel—God's good news of the sal-vation available to those who believe in the crucified and risen

Savior—is too narrow. In Kirk's view, there is an essential political and economic dimension to God's kingdom and to the gospel. This indispensable dimension turns out to be Kirk's own peculiar brand of socialism.

If one accepts Kirk's thesis, it follows that anyone who disagrees with his economic and political views—in short, anyone who supports capitalism—cannot simply be treated as an erring believer who needs instruction in basic economics; one must be regarded as a heretic, since the error touches the very core of the kingdom message.

Kirk's opposition to the kinds of economic freedom that are essential to a free society is abundantly clear. He claims that it is inconsistent with the gospel to allow people's holdings to result from the natural outworking of free exchange. The state must determine when people have accumulated too much. When that point is reached, the state is to take any excess and redistribute it among the poor, in the meantime skimming off enough to keep the agents of the state from worrying about their own standard of living. According to Kirk, the Bible teaches that any accumulation of wealth above what is absolutely required for the necessities of life must result from violence, fraud, bribes, or theft. No one in Kirk's universe ever prospers honorably.

In Kirk's "just" society, someone—he does not say who—will set both minimum and maximum pay for every job. In other words, the state will forcibly prevent anyone from working at a particular job at less than the officially set salary. Fortunately, any pain resulting from this coercion will be eased by unemployment benefits to match this minimum pay. Kirk says nothing about the economic disincentives such a program will necessarily hold for workers. He is silent about the effect on working people whose income will be forcibly taken from them by the state and redistributed in the way he describes.

All money earned above the maximum wage in Kirk's state will be "given" to charity. Naturally, before any of this money is *given* to charity, the state will have to *take* it from others. This statist appropriation of people's holdings will be aided, Kirk tells us, by "steeply progressive" tax rates. Liberals ignore the fact that statist actions like these amount to governmentally sanctioned theft. While Kirk recognizes that many people may resist the statist tyranny he proposes, he studiously avoids telling us what will be done to those who resist.

The entire scheme is so bizarre that it is difficult to believe that Kirk has really done much reflecting about his recommendations or their consequences. He makes it quite clear that such policies are required by any "Christian" approach to economics. But it would be difficult to think of a set of ideas more in conflict with sound economic thinking. The massive problems connected with his so-called Christian socialism go far beyond its restraints on personal liberty and its enhancement of the powers of the state. Minimal reflection about the effect such proposals would have on people's incentive and the long-term damage they would do to a nation's economy is enough to show Kirk's need to get in closer touch with the real world. Then again, his theorizing proves once again how easily leftist opinions collapse into utopianism.

Kirk regards people as sinners when they take risks and end up among the few who prosper. By contrast, he sees the agents of the coercive state, whose own salaries come from the monies they take from productive citizens, as presumably free from sin because they are working in the interest of the less fortunate members of society.

Kirk presents Marxism "as a strong defender of the dignity of human beings." Under Marxism, Kirk believes, "Every person has a right to develop himself freely and enjoy the fruit of his work." Marxism has "a deep compassion for people. Unlike present political systems—big business, even the Church, [Marxism] does not seem to have any particular vested interests to defend." Moreover, Marxism "contains a strong element of hope. . . . Marxism's crowning assertion is that Communist society is the only place where man can find his own real humanity by discovering that of his neighbor."[9] So Kirk does not simply praise an effete form of democratic-socialism; he lauds communism.

People who have had conversations with Kirk since the collapse of communism in Eastern Europe and the Soviet Union tell me that he appears embarrassed by material in this 1985 book. It is interesting to see how often the evangelical Left of today wants people to forget its cherished convictions of yesterday. Both Míguez Bonino's and Kirk's books stand as testaments to the radical nature of evangelical Left thinking in the recent past. Many academicians and church leaders followed in their train.

THE THREE FACES OF MARXISM

To say that someone is a Marxist, however, does not necessarily mean that the person is antidemocratic or even a revolutionary (in the violent sense of the word). It is important, both in general and for the purposes of this book, to distinguish among major schools of Marxist thought and practice.

When people identify themselves as Marxists these days, they may mean any one of a number of things. The basic varieties of Marxism have become so incompatible that advocates of the different versions fight among themselves as to which is the true Marxism. In the order in which they appeared, the three dominant versions of Marxism are (1) social democratic Marxism; (2) Marxism-Leninism; and (3) neo-Marxism (sometimes known as "humanistic Marxism").[10]

Social Democratic Marxism

For several decades after Karl Marx's death in 1883, a number of people in Great Britain taught that his ideas were compatible with democracy and political freedom. They believed that the "revolution" Marx and his colleague Friedrich Engels wrote about could be realized through peaceful means such as democratic elections. After the word "Marxism" was captured by such advocates of violent revolution as Lenin and Stalin in the twentieth century, many social democratic Marxists in Great Britain and the United States preferred to be known simply as socialists.

Social democratic Marxism was the dominant view among members of the Old Left.[11] It has been popular among many politically liberal mainline Protestants and has had growing fascination for evangelical liberals disaffected by the extremism of more radical leftists.

Marxism-Leninism

The second major interpretation of Marx was the brainchild of Lenin. As a crucial deviation from the social democratic view held by the Russian socialists known as the Mensheviks, Lenin's view became the official position of his party, the Bolsheviks. Lenin used his theories to justify the Communist Revolution of October 1917 that overthrew the democratic Mensheviks. There is no place for democracy in Lenin's version of Marxism. For Lenin, the Communists knew what was best for the workers, whether or not they agreed with the conclusions of the party.

Marxism-Leninism is totalitarian by definition. Wherever Lenin's understanding of Marx was established, it was preceded by a period of violent revolution. Castro's Cuba is a good example of Leninism in action. Nicaragua is another, where the Marxist-Leninist Sandinistas were forced by the power of the Roman Catholic church to mollify the policies they would have preferred to implement. After the breakup of the New Left movement in America, many of its more radical members gravitated toward a Leninist position.

Neo-Marxism

Neo-Marxism, or humanistic Marxism, represents a decisive departure from the first two varieties of Marxism. Perhaps the defining doctrine of neo-Marxism is the idea of alienation. Neo-Marxists claim that several unpublished early (1843–44) writings by Marx identify four different but related forms of worker alienation. It is important to note, however, that the real author of the contemporary version of the doctrine is Herbert Marcuse, the philosophical hero of student radicals in the 1960s and 1970s.

The first kind of alienation noted by Marcuse is capitalism's supposed role in causing workers to become estranged from that which they produce. Because capitalism creates false needs and provides false satisfactions, workers are manipulated into wanting things and then seduced into buying them. The workers become dominated and controlled by the things they are compelled to make.

Second, capitalism causes workers to become alienated from the labor process itself. Of course, it takes little effort to note how many men and women hate their jobs. This alienation is not restricted to those who must labor at menial, repetitive, boring, dirty, or degrading tasks. Even philosophers and professional golfers have been known to hold an occasional loathing for their jobs. It is easy to see, therefore, how people who become aware of this second form of alienation can believe that the neo-Marxists may have stumbled onto something. The catch, however, is that hating one's job is hardly unique to people who live under capitalism. It is difficult to believe that a garbage collector in Moscow is any happier with his job than a garbage collector in Boston, Cleveland, or Beverly Hills.

Third, workers under capitalism become alienated from other men and women, a fact easily observed by noting the widespread competitiveness, hostility, and animosity among human beings. Proponents of neo-Marxism want us to believe that all manifestations of these traits in the modern world can be blamed on capitalism. This claim is easily disproved by visitng any Marxist state in the world.

Fourth, workers not only become estranged from what they produce, from their work, and from other workers, but finally become alienated from themselves. This kind of alienation is manifested in many different ways, such as depression and other forms of mental illness.

I do not wish to minimize the significance of any of these forms of human alienation; all of them are serious. But it is difficult to see why Marx should be given any credit for discovering the problem or for recommending a solution. For one thing, the theory of alienation is neither unique to Marx nor original with him. The idea can be found in a number of thinkers before him, and it was developed independently by several writers after him.

Moreover, human alienation is hardly unique to capitalist societies. It simply is not true that alienation and dehumanization result exclusively from conditions existing in capitalist societies and vanish once those societies have become socialist. Human alienation is no more an exclusive effect of capitalism than baldness.

This Marcusian brand of Marxism happens to have been the majority opinion of the evangelical Left. While it is not always clear whether members of the Religious Left have actually read Marcuse, they obviously fail to understand the serious theoretical weaknesses of his system.

Indeed, strangely missing from the thinking of Christian neo-Marxists is recognition of a fifth variety of human alienation, a type that Marx also conveniently ignored. Scripture teaches that every member of the human race is *alienated from God*. In fact, the Bible clearly implies that all the forms of human alienation cited by the neo-Marxists result in some way from mankind's more fundamental alienation from its Creator. Recognition of this biblical truth could have a profound impact on Christian neo-Marxists and might even diminish the enthusiasm of sociology professors in Christian colleges for what they mistakenly regard as the core of Marx's teaching.

Marcuse's ideas appear to have affected many people emotionally. They use the terminology, and they have surrendered to his ideology. But when challenged, they usually lack the finesse necessary to defend that system. This is often the way ideologies work.

TONY CAMPOLO'S FAVORITE MARXIST

In the meantime, neo-Marxism still has a significant influence on some Christian campuses. About fifteen years ago I participated in a conference with a group of people who teach sociology at various evangelical schools. After just an hour or so (long enough for everyone around the table to speak), it became obvious that everyone else in the room was a neo-Marxist. Their professional training in sociology had so indoctrinated them in Herbert Marcuse's style of socialism that they were incapable of talking about their discipline without using Marcuse's categories and assumptions. Their entire approach to sociology—their "understanding" of the world—was controlled by neo-Marxist presuppositions. I saw no indication that these Christian sociologists were even aware of the powerful philosophical and economic arguments against the views they accepted so uncritically.[12]

Sociologist Tony Campolo provides unwitting support for these claims. He spends three chapters of his book *Partly Right* praising Karl Marx for what he regards as Marx's important claims about human alienation.[13] Astute readers will recognize similar views in some of Campolo's other books.[14] Campolo's writings show no awareness of the fact that the real source of the views he praises is Marcuse, not Marx.[15] In fact, Campolo seems unaware of the strange circumstances that brought Marx's early unpublished writings to the place where they became a major influence on Christian thinkers like him.

Marx's early writings were not published until 1932. In the setting of the early 1930s, the 1843–44 manuscripts seemed to reveal a Marx quite different from the version favored by Lenin and Stalin. For people weary of or frightened by the ruthless tyranny of Stalin, publication of the early manuscripts made it possible to appeal to the authority of Marx in defense of individual human dignity and freedom. Predictably, early proponents of this view in the Soviet Union either were forced to recant publicly or simply disappeared.

After World War II, this new Marx became especially appealing to intellectuals in the captive nations of Eastern Europe. Marxism-Leninism's contempt for human rights gave added incentive to find a Marx whose name and authority could be used to bring about a restoration of humanitarian concerns in the brutal conditions that prevailed under Stalin. What began in Eastern Europe as an attempt to find an acceptable basis for humanism within a Marxist context became in the West a new way of glorifying Marx, which is precisely what we find in Campolo's book.

When Marcuse's life and university position were threatened by the Nazis in the 1930s, he fled his native Germany and came to America, where he eventually ended up as a philosophy professor at the University of California at San Diego. During World War II, however, he worked for the Office of Strategic Services (OSS), the forerunner to today's Central Intelligence Agency (CIA). It is unlikely that Marcuse's adoring followers in the radical Left fully understood his relationship to America's hated spy agency. But perhaps they didn't care, since Marcuse used his connections to help Marxist allies gain positions of influence and power in the postwar German government.

Even though Marx's early unpublished writings served as a foundation for Marcuse's system, he used them to justify his own peculiar brand of totalitarianism.[16] Marcuse acknowledged the deceit behind claims that socialism expands human liberty. Even the socialist who dreams of a socialist democracy at the end of the transformation of society must assent to the use of repressive measures against any who would impede his noble goals. It should come as no surprise that the kind of dictatorship Marcuse envisioned would be one in which he and his followers become the ruling elite.

Campolo seems uninformed about all this. Moreover, he and other devotees of the humanistic reading of Marx fail to see how their theory suffers from enormous problems. One jarring consequence of the humanistic interpretation is its implication that no one really understood Marx until 1932. Serious scholars recognize that Marx later abandoned the rambling comments about human alienation that appeared in his earlier writings; his mature writings are totally incompatible with neo-Marxist thinking.[17] It is difficult to believe that Campolo would have praised Marx so effusively had he been aware of this fact.

When these weaknesses are understood, humanistic Marxism can be seen to rest on a questionable interpretation of questionable writings that are the basis of a questionable theory that, in all likelihood, Marx himself repudiated. The Marcusian Marxism of Campolo and large numbers of Christian sociologists is a system built on quicksand.

CONCLUSION

The information in the last two chapters poses a major hurdle for anyone naive enough to think that the current leaders of the evangelical Left represent a centrist-moderate position. Many of them have been proponents of far-left theories or have been close associates of advocates of such ideas.

Chapter Five

Jim Wallis and the Sojourners Movement

Jim Wallis is the super-radical of the Evangelical Triumvirate.[1] People who have never been attracted to political radicalism find it difficult to think Wallis's thoughts after him. Wallis used to get his clout from his monthly magazine *Sojourners*, which is now published every other month because of declining numbers of subscribers.

Wallis entered Michigan State University during the sixties after leaving his family's Plymouth Brethren congregation near Detroit because of what he describes as racism. Instead of repudiating the entire Christian faith, some critics have suggested, a more rational person would have simply transferred to a less bigoted church. But Wallis has always been less tolerant of inconsistent Christians than of erring non-Christian leftists, no matter how badly the latter behave.

During his college years, Wallis joined Students for a Democratic Society (SDS), one of the more radical movements of the time. When the New Left began to fall apart in the late sixties, Wallis once again embraced the Christian faith. But in doing so, he still clung to the antiwar, anti-American attitudes and radical beliefs he had acquired in his New Left days. After the breakup of the SDS, many of Wallis's radical colleagues began to drift back into the mainstream of American life. Some became stockbrokers, real estate agents, or insurance salesmen. Wallis, by contrast, decided to juggle religion and far-left politics in a way different from anyone before or since. After all, the religion Wallis professed was the mature evangelicalism that had developed out of the fundamentalism of the first half of the twentieth century. Wallis's writings since that time suggest, as K. L. Billingsley observes, "that Karl Marx was part of the deal and that the new evangelical mission was to liberate the church from the evils of capitalism."[2]

Wallis himself has made this point by noting that

> As more Christians become influenced by liberation theology, finding themselves increasingly rejecting the values and institutions of capitalism, they will also be drawn to the Marxist analysis and praxis that is so central to the movement. That more Christians will come to view the world through Marxist eyes is therefore predictable. It will even be predictable among the so-called 'young evangelicals' who, for the most part, have a zeal for social change that is not yet matched by a developed socio-economic analysis that will cause them to see the impossibility of making capitalism work for justice and peace.[3]

While studying at Trinity Evangelical Divinity School in the early 1970s, Wallis and some allies at the school began publishing a mimeographed magazine called *The Post-American*. The cover of the first issue contained a picture of Jesus in Pilate's judgment hall and dressed only in an American flag. The most prominent words on that cover were "The Bitch Goddess of Capitalism." The impact of the total picture was obvious: Faithful Christians will have nothing to do with either America or capitalism.

In 1976 Wallis made improvements to his magazine and changed its name to *Sojourners*. He also moved himself and his magazine to Washington, D.C., where he founded a small community, also called the Sojourners.

WALLIS AND VIETNAM

While Wallis portrayed himself and his publication as antiwar, he was noticeably silent about the warlike invasion of South Vietnam by the North Vietnamese army. Wallis responded to the American withdrawal and the North Vietnamese takeover with these words:

> It's over, thank God it's over. I don't know how else to express the quiet emotion that rushed through me when the news reports showed that the United States had finally been defeated in Vietnam. There was an overwhelming sense of relief and thankfulness that the American intruders had finally been thrown out and that the desire of the U.S. government to control the destiny of Indochina had been thwarted.[4]

Bui Tin, the general of the North Vietnamese Army who accepted South Vietnam's surrender, recently admitted that antiwar protestors like Jim Wallis and other members of the Religious Left at the time "undermined the American war effort and . . . gave aid and comfort to the enemy."[5] In the words of the general, the antiwar protestors "represented the conscience of America." That conscience, he continued, "was part of its war-making capability, and we [the North Vietnamese] were turning that power in our favor."[6] Commenting on this, an editorial in *National Review* observed that while the anti-Vietnam war protestors

> didn't cause the war . . . they weakened our will to continue, resulting in our broken promise to the people of South Vietnam and—lest we forget—to the 57,000 Americans who died there. The Sixties pacifists can atone for their past offenses by admitting what their professions of peace-and-love led to.[7]

The leaders of postwar Vietnam were Stalinists, that is, expansionist revolutionary totalitarians. They were far more repressive than their sponsors in Moscow. Another early opponent of the Vietnam War, Richard John Neuhaus, protested publicly against the outrageous violations of human rights perpetrated by the Hanoi regime. Jim Wallis responded by attacking Neuhaus and others who dared to criticize the North Vietnamese.[8]

During the Hanoi regime's worst oppression in 1976, Wallis's implacable anti-Americanism led him to write that even though the antiwar movement had passed from the scene, its opposition to the American war in Vietnam had now been thoroughly vindicated. In Wallis's words,

> What antiwar activists said about the nature and purposes of American war policy have been shown to be true.... In Vietnam, the U.S. government exposed itself as an essentially lawless and predatory regime. The criminal destruction of a whole people and their way of life was a deliberate policy choice made to secure American economic and military objectives in Southeast Asia. It is not a rhetorical ploy, but a statement of fact, to charge that the American government and the American people are guilty of war crimes comparable in substance, if not in scope, to the offenses of German leaders in the 1930s and 40s.[9]

This immoral ploy of suggesting similarities between America and the Nazis has been typical of the radical far Left. This page from Wallis's past—a page he has never repudiated—puts his compulsive anti-Americanism out in the open.

Those Wicked People Who Fled Communist Vietnam

After the American withdrawal, hundreds of thousands of people fled Vietnam, many of them dying in the attempt. Wallis's view of such people at the time is worthy of notice. In a 1979 *Sojourners* piece, he suggested that the refugees fleeing Indochina had been "inoculated with a taste for Western lifestyle." They were escaping, Wallis claimed,

> to support their consumer habit in other lands.... The burden of responsibility for the refugees falls heavily on the United States.... We must not support the boat people as a way of vindicating ourselves and showing Vietnam to be a bad country after all.... Ours must be an informed response

that does not play into the hands of our government's desire to further discredit and isolate Vietnam.[10]

In other words, as Paul Hollander explains, the Vietnamese boat people

> were suffering from false consciousness and fleeing for unworthy reasons which reflected their own moral corruption. The alleged corruption and untrustworthiness of refugees from communist countries has been a long-standing claim among those reluctant to allow their testimony to be weighed in the indictment of these systems.... It was difficult for the critics of American society to forgive the refugees for risking their lives to enter a country the critics held in deep contempt. At the same time, information originating with the officials of the countries the refugees fled, including Vietnam, was deemed reliable as it coincided with the preconception of the critics.[11]

Let us remember that we are examining Wallis's explanation of why so many Vietnamese left their country in dangerous and overcrowded boats, many of them destined to drown at sea or be raped, robbed, and killed by pirates. Wallis compared these poor people to addicts fleeing to another land in order to support a drug habit. Billingsley writes:

> Imagine this scenario: You are a Vietnamese refugee, drifting on a derelict freighter in the South China Sea. Water is low; food almost nonexistent. You have no medical supplies or resources of any sort. Speedboats appear, full of heavily armed Thai pirates who rape the younger women, take some prisoners, steal everything they can find, murder some people outright, then sink the ship. You are left treading water, the cries of the drowning ringing in your ears. Wouldn't it be comforting to know that in secure, faraway America, the editor of a radical magazine, in an editorial about compassion, is announcing to the world that you are a Western junkie, fleeing to support your consumer habit in other lands?[12]

Wallis's response to the Cambodian Communists' slaughter of two million men, women, and children was to deny the bloodbath and blame whatever else might happen on the United States.[13] So much for compassion for poor and oppressed people. So much for someone claiming to be a "peace and justice Christian."

RICHARD BARNETT AND THE INSTITUTE FOR POLICY STUDIES

Much can be learned by observing the people who became Wallis's allies during the 1980s. One of them was Richard Barnett, whom Billingsley describes as "a left-wing anti-capitalist intellectual and co-founder of the radical think tank, the Institute for Policy Studies" (IPS).[14] Rael and Erich Isaac identify Barnett's institute as the major think tank of the coercive utopians in America.[15] Paul Hollander warns that IPS is known "for its capacity to accommodate many varieties of leftism and to nurture virtually every adversarial current in American society during the past quarter-century. It has exemplified the durability of the radical-critical sensibility and exerted considerable influence on what used to be the liberal side of the political spectrum."[16] Billingsley cites sources that identify IPS "as an interlocking directorate of the American Left as well as a longtime hangout for Eastern Bloc diplomats, KGB agents, pro-Castro propagandists like Sol Landau, and misunderstood liberals like Alger Hiss."[17]

Hollander notes the close ties between Sojourners and the Institute of Policy Studies.[18] For one thing, Barnett and other leftists encouraged Wallis to move his operation to Washington, D.C., the site of their institute. For another, Barnett became an editor of *Sojourners*. Hollander details the clever ways IPS established secret ties to other leftist organizations, some of them offshoots of its own operation. Many apparently independent organizations that have influenced Congress and the media along leftist lines were in fact funded by IPS money.

Questions have been raised about Wallis's own sources of funding. During the 1980s many fine evangelical publications such as *Eternity* went under because of inadequate funding and declining subscribers. But while other publications were failing, *Sojourners'* very expensive operation continued to expand. Where did Wallis's operation get the resources? Billingsley reports that Wallis sought a grant in the late 1980s that required him to complete a questionnaire listing the names of other *Sojourners* supporters. Two names on Wallis's list were the Pillsbury Corporation and Joan Kroc, the liberal heiress of the founder of McDonald's. But the contributor Billingsley finds most intriguing was Cora Weiss, whom he describes as "the daughter of Samuel Rubin, a Communist Party member who used his Faberge cosmetics fortune to establish the Institute for Policy Studies."[19]

It would appear that Wallis's operation was assisted by organizations that had lots of money to give away but little interest in his religious convictions. It is easy to wonder whether at least some of them saw Sojourners as a way of getting their message across to unsuspecting religious people.

We do not know fully what connections existed between Sojourners and the Institute for Policy Studies, but we do know that he opened the pages of his magazine to IPS officials such as Richard Barnett.

WALLIS'S FONDNESS FOR THE SOVIET UNION

Wallis consistently displayed a support for the Soviet Union and its actions that was all too reminiscent of IPS's own public pronouncements. K. L. Billingsley reminds us, "The Soviets and their Cuban foreign legion were on a roll in Angola, Mozambique, Ethiopia, and other hot spots in the early '80s. Pro-Soviet guerillas were gaining strength in Latin America."[20] Wallis refused to criticize the Soviet invasion of Afghanistan. In the ideology of Wallis and his pro-Soviet friends, it was America that posed the greatest threat to world peace. Wallis, like other leftists, was a strong proponent of the doctrine of moral equivalence. As Billingsley describes it, "there was no practical difference between dictatorship and democracy, between freedom and unfreedom."[21]

When the pro-Soviet leaders of Poland imposed martial law because of efforts to establish the first independent trade union in the Communist bloc, Wallis remained silent about the oppression and found a way to attack the American government's motives in condemning the repression in Poland.[22] As Billingsley observes, radical Leftists like Wallis believe that "only America and the West commit 'sins' and are judged by their record. On the other hand, leftist regimes are judged by their rhetoric and intentions, not by the disasters they create. They make only the occasional 'blunders.'"[23]

Even though Soviet Premier Leonid Brezhnev was a tyrant who persecuted his enemies with a ferocity excessive even by Soviet standards, his death provided Wallis with an occasion for eulogizing this evil man. In Wallis's words, "If we could not call Brezhnev a peacemaker, we could at least recognize him as a moderate man, a man open to reason."[24] Wallis's eulogy contained no mention of Soviet leader Leonid Brezhnev's orders to invade Afghanistan or to deploy SS–20 missiles or to repress Andrei Sakharov and other dissidents. Instead, Wallis portrayed Brezhnev as a man who really wanted peace. Wallis even described a prayer meeting he attended following Brezhnev's death at which Wallis and others asked forgiveness for America's anti-communism.[25]

The Doctrine of Moral Equivalence

Wallis's commitment to the moral equivalence of the United States and the U.S.S.R., which he affirms in his book *Agenda for Biblical People*,[26] requires additional comment. When the Soviet Union was still a political entity, the Religious Left in the U.S. followed the lead of the secular Left in espousing the doctrine of moral equivalence. Dean Curry, a professor of government at Messiah College, notes that this was the belief

that the United States and the Soviet Union [were] two similar kinds of nations. Both ... systems [were] repressive and both of their foreign policies [were] characterized by brutality as they [sought] to exploit and dominate others. In short, in terms of their motivations and their actions, the conclusion [was] drawn that both nations [were] morally equivalent.[27]

On this view of things, there were no moral differences between the United States and the Soviet Union. Under no conditions could the U.S. be seen as morally superior to the old Soviet Union, nor could it possibly make a bit of difference which nation might win or lose the cold war. According to Paul Hollander, "Even when the so-called moral equivalence thesis is ostensibly applied [by left-wing critics], to the United States and its adversaries, in particular the Soviet Union, it soon becomes clear that it is the United States that bears the brunt of the criticism and especially its emotional sting."[28]

Of course, now that the Soviet Union has dissolved and the leaders of the new Russia have opened the files of their military and secret police, the evidence is there to disprove the doctrine of moral equivalence. Along with these revelations come ample expressions of Russian shame at what previous leaders did to innocent Soviet citizens as well as to innocent people in other nations. Since the collapse of communism, many members of the Religious Left in the United States would like their former defense of moral equivalence to be forgotten.

The Shooting Down of Flight 007

It is interesting to note Wallis's reaction to the Soviets' shooting down of Korean Airlines Flight 007 in August 1982, a deed that killed 269 people. *Sojourners* writer Danny Collum reported this as a "tragic blunder" that the Soviets then followed with a "callous coverup."[29] But *Sojourners* had more to say. "Soviet leaders," Collum continued, "were genuinely and understandably bewildered by the unusually vicious and frenzied name-calling that came from the United States in the wake of the tragedy."[30] Note how use of the word "tragedy" serves to cleanse the atrocity of any moral blame. This response was made to an intentional, cold-blooded act of murder, ordered by Soviet leaders against 269 innocent people. Wallis found a way to also blame the United States.

However, we must all be extremely careful lest we become so self-righteous in our own indignation and anger over this incident that we become guilty of hypocrisy. The root causes of these tragic deaths are to be found in the pervasive climate of fear, distrust, and hostility that has been allowed to develop among many nations. But in particular, the poisoned relations between ourselves and the Soviet Union have created a virtual war mentality. The passengers aboard flight 007 were clear victims of that mentality. The Soviet Union is responsible for the murders of these people, but we must also share the guilt. On such a dark day, none of us is innocent.[31]

Billingsley justly denounces Wallis's outrageous declaration. "If Wallis feels guilty for an act perpetrated by the Soviet government, that is his problem. I do not feel any such guilt; I feel outrage. To tell the relatives of these murdered people—many of them children—that 'we must also share the guilt,' can hardly be construed as a message of comfort."[32]

Wallis and Latin American Communism

When the Soviet Union attempted to export its influence into Central America in the 1980s, Wallis's support was evident. According to Billingsley, Wallis and his magazine have been strong supporters of Fidel Castro and his tyrannical rule over Cuba.[33] Wallis thought the Nicaraguan Sandinistas were good people who were committed to helping the poor. The Sandinista persecution of Miskito Indians was dismissed as simply an error in judgment.[34] *Sojourners* once devoted an entire month's issue to celebrate Marxist Nicaguarua.[35] Not surprisingly, Wallis has been silent about the way the Sandinistas robbed Nicaragua following their electoral defeat in 1990, as we observed in chapter 3.

WALLIS'S ANTI-AMERICANISM

It should be no surprise that Wallis appears prominently in the pages of Paul Hollander's book *Anti-Americanism*. K. L. Billingsley notes that "In spite of all that has happened since the '60s, the Rev. Jim Wallis still nurtures his cherished hatreds for the United States and its people. He apparently believes that the United States, not Saddam Hussein, invaded Kuwait, and claims to have fasted for 47 days over the Gulf War."[36]

In a 1987 book edited by Wallis, two contributors compare American trains transporting nuclear weapons to the trains that carried European Jews to the gas chambers in Nazi concentration camps.[37] Commenting on such claims, Hollander explains that the goals of such American leftists has been "to inflame moral indignation by associating current American policies with those of Nazi Germany and, second, to legitimate civil disobedience, or what amounted to sabotaging the military policies of the country."[38]

WALLIS AND EVANGELICALISM

While the early issues of *Sojourners* assured Wallis's readers that his publication was going to be something new—a committed integration of evangelical belief and a concern for social justice—something happened along the way. In fact, it happened about the time he upgraded his magazine and moved. It occurred about the time he began to invite Richard Barnett of IPS, the radical priest Daniel Berrigan, and others of their persuasion to write for him. The evangelical content of Wallis's magazine began to diminish considerably. Perhaps he did not want to offend the secular leftists and the theologically liberal Protestants and Catholics, who by then made up a sizable share of his readers,[39] by dealing with matters of theology and doctrine such as the new birth and personal salvation.

By contrast, he has continued to attack conservative Christians at will. In *The Rise of Christian Conscience,* Wallis equated American fundamentalists with the Ayatollahs of Iran.[40] The biggest target of his wrath is the Christian Right. According to Wallis, the Religious Right "has been a white religion, has fueled the backlash against women's rights, and has used blatant caricatures and attacks on homosexuals as highly successful fund-raising techniques. The confusion and rejection of Christian faith caused by this unholy alliance of religious appeals and right-wing politics are now pervasive."[41]

One wonders how Wallis dares accuse others of using blatant caricatures and stereotypes. It is also ironic to see him offended by conservatives whom he describes as pursuing an "unholy alliance of religion and politics," an act of which he himself is guilty, albeit while operating under a different set of convictions.

Wallis also makes clear his disdain of the popular coinage "family values." "The rhetoric of family values," he writes, "has become especially pernicious."[42] He twists criticisms of families without a live-in father into some kind of patriarchal conspiracy. He ignores the harm caused by absent fathers. He is silent about the fact that most of these matriarchal families result from irresponsible, immoral, and faithless men moving on and leaving behind their illegitimate children. He ignores the complicity of the liberal welfare state and liberal politicians in encouraging the appalling rates of illegitimacy now sweeping the United States. His only response to this condition is to denounce those who seek to restore the biblical view of the home to its former place of prominence in American society.

CONCLUSION

One disturbing aspect of Jim Wallis's political convictions is his current claim to be recognized as a centrist or moderate. My evaluation of this assertion is the focus of the next chapter.

Chapter Six

Up Against the Wallis

This continuation of my investigation into the views of Jim Wallis contains four parts. First, I examine the testimony of evangelical theologian Clark Pinnock and the light it throws on Wallis's views. Second, I explore Wallis's relationship to a strange publication called *The Road to Damascus*. Third, I take a brief look at a 1994 book in which Wallis makes a major appeal to be recognized as a centrist or moderate. Finally, I review one or two more recent essays just to see whether the remade Wallis has anything new to say. All this material throws additional light on Wallis's claim to be a new kind of centrist.

CLARK PINNOCK'S ACCOUNT OF THE EVANGELICAL LEFT

One telling revelation of the true nature of the Religious Left has come from one of its early founders, evangelical theologian Clark H. Pinnock. Pinnock was not only present at the birth of what became the Sojourners movement, but also served on the magazine's editorial board for several years.

Clark Pinnock is a well-known and much published evangelical author. He has taught at New Orleans Baptist Theological Seminary, Trinity Evangelical Divinity School, and Regent College and is at present professor of theology at McMaster Divinity School in Canada. What is not so well-known is that during the early 1970s, while teaching at Trinity in Deerfield, Illinois, Pinnock became part of Jim Wallis's radical Left movement at the school.

Pinnock describes his support for the radical Left in those early years as the result of a kind of political conversion. In 1970, he explains, his "political thinking underwent a paradigm shift—a total transformation." He found himself looking at society from the perspective we now call the New Left. He came to believe that the Bible obliged him to reject anything connected with democratic capitalism. "It was," he explains, "a new political-theological world to move in and it produced a heady experience which intoxicated me and many others. It led me personally to sympathy and support for the Marxist movements of the world."[1]

Pinnock describes the attraction that socialism had for him and others in the movement. He thought that socialism was

> a grand vision of a just and humane order which distributed its resources fairly and equitably among all its people according to their need.... Without equating the two, it was so easy for me to associate in my mind the socialist utopia and the promised kingdom of God.... We admired what we thought was happening in the new China under Mao, and we hoped that the Viet Cong would win out against American forces.[2]

Although he remained associated with the movement even after Wallis moved to Washington, Pinnock eventually felt new opinions stirring within him. "Gradually, I began to reassess my position and my alienation from North America began to fade, replaced by a certain critical appreciation of democratic capitalism that I had had before 1970."[3] He recalls someone's asking him whether he realized how much Marxism could be found within the pages of *Sojourners*. Up to that point it had not occurred to him that so much of what the magazine and the movement stood for represented a Marxist worldview.

Pinnock explains what finally brought him to his senses:

> It now struck me as somewhat ridiculous to overlook those positive features of North American life which had incidentally made it possible for radicals like me to express and live

out our concerns. How could I have had such deep contempt for a culture which surely stands as a beacon of hope in this suffering world? How ironic to call for "liberation" in the very place there is probably more of it than anywhere else in the world, and to be sympathetic toward those societies where neither liberty nor justice is in good supply. It began to dawn on me that if one was looking for Babylon in this present world, one might rather look toward the threat of totalitarian government.[4]

Pinnock changed his mind, about both the United States and communism. "What really endangers liberty and justice in our world," he wrote, "is not a flawed America, but that political monism, whether of the fascist right or the Communist left, which declares itself to be absolute and answers to no transcendent value."[5]

He also changed his mind about democratic capitalism. "Far from being the enemy of the poor," he wrote, capitalism "now seems to me to offer both liberty and prosperity in abundance and to deserve our cautious support. Socialism, on the other hand, has a dismal record of providing neither."[6]

Pinnock's candid confession is a powerful exposé of the workings of the radical mind. The tragedy is that every year large numbers of Christian young people who know nothing about Pinnock's pilgrimage are seduced through similar arguments offered by professors on college campuses. The Religious Left keeps rolling along, oblivious to the powerful economic and philosophic cases that has been mustered against it.

Jim Wallis and others in the Religious Left claim to be part of an ideologically pure, nonpolitical movement that has supposedly arisen from a fresh reading of the Bible. But, their critics point out, the far-left extremists have not been faithful to the social message of the Scriptures. They have simply surrendered to the prevailing ideology of the political Left and have read the content of *that* message into God's Word.

THE ROAD TO DAMASCUS DOCUMENT

Jim Wallis's efforts to portray himself as a moderate is contradicted by many of his past actions and statements. A notable example of this was the publication in 1989 of an unusual twenty-eight-page document titled *The Road to Damascus*. Wallis and the Sojourners organization served as the American distributor of the publication. While no authors of the document were named, signers represented seven nations: the Philippines, South Korea, Namibia, South Africa, El Salvador, Nicaragua, and Guatemala. All the signers were leftists from nations where Marxist efforts to consolidate left-wing movements were resisted by people who were concerned about the aid such Marxists have given to proponents of violence and totalitarianism.

In language designed to assert simultaneously their own virtue and the alleged wickedness of their critics, the writers of *The Road to Damascus* described themselves as representatives of a "Christian theology that sides with the poor and oppressed."[7] But what the signers understood by "following Christ" is not what the apostle Paul understood. They used words like "idolatry," "heresy," "apostasy," and "blasphemy" to describe failure to support the Marxist causes they espoused. The good people in this struggle include proponents of liberation theology, black theology, and radical feminist theology. The bad people include any Christians who resist and oppose the efforts of the Christian Marxists.

To make certain that the point won't be missed, the document identifies "anti-Communist evangelicals" as members of the forces of darkness.[8] In other words, good Christians must be pro-Communist; anti-Communists are bad Christians. Anti-Communist Christians are like Saint Paul before his conversion: enemies of Christ and of the Christian faith. The document calls them to conversion—a conversion to Marxism.

The Damascus document was a politically partisan test of what constitutes Christian faithfulness. George Weigel, one of the first to criticize it, objected that it offers us nothing less than a political-economic test of Christian fidelity, failing which one is declared, simply, excommunicate: beyond the boundaries of the Body of Christ. Differing views on politics and economics are, in other words, raised above one's affirmation of the classic Christian doctrines (the Trinity, grace, the Incarnation) as the point of division between believers and nonbelievers or, as the document itself puts it, between true Christians and apostates.[9]

Almost as astounding as what the document said was the absence of any controversy over it among members of the evangelical and Catholic Left. After all, Richard John Neuhaus pointed out, the document dared to suggest that

> a new church has been founded, The People's Church of the Anti-Imperialist Struggle. According to this document, "the truth of the Christian faith" has little or nothing to do with faith in Christ, Scripture, or the classic creeds, and everything to do with a socio-economic analysis of class struggle. The creedal key ... is "the preferential option for the poor."[10]

Neuhaus branded as shameful the silence of supposedly responsible Christians in the United States who tried to act as if the document never existed and was not promoted by Jim Wallis and the Sojourners.

It must be remembered that *The Road to Damascus* appeared just weeks before the anti-Communist movements in the Soviet Union and the People's Republic of China began to change the world order and the political map. That makes Weigel's criticism all the more fitting:

> The time is long past when those who most loudly proclaim their "preferential option for the poor" should be given the benefit of the doubt. The world has learned some things about poverty and wealth, development and underdevelopment, these last few decades or so. We have learned that human resources and capital are as important, and probably more important, than natural resources. We have

learned that market-oriented economies are far more likely to raise the poor's standard of living than state-centered or command economies. We have learned that the entrepreneurial energies of the people of the Third World are being strangled by a thick net of mercantilist and modern statist regulations. We have learned that post-independence dictators in the Third World are often more corrupt than their former colonial masters. We have learned that aggregate amounts of foreign aid are no index of successful development in the recipient nation. And we have learned that when people are actually given the choice, they inevitably opt for the kinds of economies that allow them to function as free economic actors.[11]

Yet, Weigel continues, "the sponsors and authors of the Damascus Document seem wholly innocent of all this."

There is no excuse for such extraordinary ignorance of empirical reality. People are ignorant of these things either because they are culpably lazy and not paying very much attention or because they find the truth ideologically unsettling.

This powerful indictment applies not only to the signers and sponsors of the Damascus Document—a group that Jim Wallis proudly identifies with—but also to the large company of outdated liberation theologians who still cling to the socialist and revolutionary dreams of the past and to their utopian fellow-travelers in American Christendom. *The Road to Damascus* document offers firm evidence that religious leftists like Jim Wallis were involved with far more than an innocent flirtation with Marxist social analysis.

JIM WALLIS, THE CENTRIST?

So far as I know, Jim Wallis was the first of the evangelical Left leadership to publish claims about his centrist stance in America's ongoing political and cultural struggle. Within a year, three major signers of *The Cry for Renewal* published books touting their centrist credentials. *Is Jesus a Republican or a Democrat?* by Tony Campolo appeared in October 1995, a few months after *Cease Fire:*

Searching for Sanity in America's Culture Wars, a similar book by Tom Sine.[12]

Wallis's work, *The Soul of Politics,*[13] was published by Orbis Books in 1994. As the publishing arm of the radical left Catholic movement known as the Maryknollers, Orbis has been the dominant U.S. source for books touting the virtues of liberation theology and other assorted efforts to integrate Christianity and Marxism.

Wallis begins his book by suggesting that he represents a stance that is somehow different from both liberalism and conservativism.[14] His second chapter carries the subtitle "Beyond Liberal and Conservative." He states that "the dominant political ideologies of liberal and conservative, Left and Right, seem equally incapable of discerning our present crisis or leading us into the future. Politics has become almost completely dysfunctional."[15] Both sides, Wallis contends, focus on different aspects of America's social crisis. "Conservatives talk endlessly about personal responsibility. . . . liberals seem to only know the language of human rights and social compassion."[16] Similar claims appear in the books by Campolo and Sine. Wallis writes:

> To speak only of moral behavior, apart from oppressive social realities, just blames the victim; and to talk only about social conditions, apart from moral choices, is to keep treating people only as victims. Only a social analysis and practice that transcends the two approaches and forges new options has any chance of succeeding in an increasingly volatile and dangerous cultural context. The culture war that is raging between the advocates of social justice and the preachers of moral rejuvenation must come to an end, not simply to make a truce between embattled intellectuals but also for the sake of our endangered children, who have become the chief pawns and victims of our absurd bifurcations.[17]

It does seem strange to focus on moral behavior in a way that separates it from oppressive social realities. One such reality—the liberal welfare state—is responsible for much of the harm done to the poor in the past thirty years; it has played a role in the decline of morality among many of its recipients. Wallis's claims that only liberals care about social justice are false and that liberal theories would effectively establish social justice are naive.

"Liberalism's best impulse," Wallis writes, "is to care about the disenfranchised and insist that a society is responsible for its people. But liberalism became captive to large distant institutions and impersonal bureaucracies that are more concerned with control than caring, and the result became more dependency than empowerment."[18]

By contrast, "Conservatism's best impulse is to stress the need for individual initative and moral responsibility. But because of its attachment to institutions of wealth and power, preference for the status quo, and the lack of a strong ethic of social responsibility, conservatism has virtually abandoned the poor and dispossessed."[19]

Wallis offers an interesting insight into his sudden dislike of Marxian ideology.

> Much idealism was lost on Marxist ideology; generations of capitalism's moral dissenters put their frail hopes in one revolutionary incarnation after another, only to be eventually betrayed. The most systematic challenge to the West finally collapsed—its best impulses having died long before—and the world was left with still no alternative to the many sins of the global corporate economy.[20]

Instead of being grateful that American persistence in the cold war led to the collapse of communism, Wallis announces that he will never forgive the Soviets because they were the world's last great hope to destroy capitalism and defeat America—and they failed. Are these the opinions of a centrist? What were those "best impulses" of the Soviet challenge to the West? Could we, for example, learn them through the testimony of the millions of people who died in the Soviet Union's Gulag Archipelago?

No issue is perhaps more baffling for liberals like Wallis than abortion. He seems to have straddled the fence. At times he sounds sympathetic to the the pro-life cause, but he also seems anxious not to do or say anything that might offend the extreme pro-abortion feminists.[21] He finally chooses to ignore this dilemma that is not resolvable on his grounds.

Based on what Wallis says in his book, he has no moral or religious objections to sodomy, but woe unto anyone who finds such behavior offensive or sinful.[22] Wallis is strangely silent about claims from both Ron Sider and Tony Campolo that homosexual behavior is sinful. Wallis condemns the Religious Right for what he calls "hate-mongering homophobia." He claims that the "outrageous" public actions of homosexual groups like "Queer Nation" are an understandable reaction to the tactics of anti-homosexuals.[23]

Nowhere in Wallis's writings can one find an examination of biblical teaching on this issue, although it is clear that Wallis sides with those who interpret Scripture in ways that make homosexual conduct innocent of biblical censure.

An interesting review of Wallis's book appeared in a 1994 issue of Ron Sider's magazine *Prism*.[24] The author, Joel Shuman, is described as an Assemblies of God minister, doctoral student at Duke University, and ally of Evangelicals for Social Action. Shuman begins his review by reverently describing Wallis's influence on his understanding of Christian discipleship.

"I was nearly certain," Shuman writes, "that Jim Wallis would be the one person who might possibly inject a moment of prophetic clarity into what seems to have become an otherwise intractable and unintelligible screaming match concerning the form a genuinely Christian politics might take."[25]

But then Shuman pauses. Wallis's book is not exactly what he had expected. This is not to say that Shuman thinks Wallis's work is defective in any way. "Perhaps it is this book's scope, which is, to say the least, ambitious: calling for nothing less than the complete transformation of geopolitics demands that an author paint with a broad brush. Or perhaps it is simply that the transformation Wallis longs for is so sweeping that he is never able to specify exactly what he wants, and from whom."[26] It is hard to believe that Shuman actually expected anything approaching this, since Wallis's book is largely a reworking of old material from *Sojourners*. Shuman's respect for Wallis keeps him from considering the more likely option, which is that Wallis does not have a clue about how to achieve this new world order.

Shuman *thinks* (but cannot be sure) that Wallis may be trying to lay out a new approach to the business of government in America. But Shuman cannot quite figure out what Wallis is about. When ideologically blinded followers of someone they regard as omniscient cannot understand the teaching of the Master, it is common for them to seek the reason for the lack of understanding in themselves. Shuman, it is clear, is looking in the wrong direction and does not recognize that the emperor has no clothes.

Shuman notes how Wallis begins his book by declaring that "The world isn't working. Things are unraveling, and most of us know it." Shuman agrees, but then suggests that "The question, however, is whether the world ever did work, and whether we should expect it to start now."[27] So even Shuman has to admit that when it comes to solutions, Wallis has nothing to say.

DOES THE "CENTRIST" WALLIS HAVE ANYTHING NEW TO SAY?

A good place to seek answers to questions about Jim Wallis's current views are two *Sojourners* essays written after his book went to press. The first article is titled "As If Values Mattered" and was published in November 1993.[28] Even though Ron Sider has uneasily acknowledged his errors about capitalism and now admits that capitalism has a necessary role to play in helping the poor, Wallis remains intransigent. He writes, "With the end of the Cold War and the collapse of communism, capitalism also requires fresh evaluation, especially in its failures in regard to both equity and ecology."[29]

Wallis's alternative to capitalism is what he calls a "community economy." And what are some specifics about this new kind of economy? Wallis finally admits that he's not quite sure. "The details of what a community economy would look like are far from clear."[30] Further, "Goods and services need to be produced, but the wealth from such production could certainly be shared more equitably than it is now."[31] This smells suspiciously like many of the old SDS and New Left schemes.

The second article, "To the Highest Bidder," was published in the November-December 1995 issue of *Sojourners*. In it, Wallis repeats a formula that all the leaders of the evangelical Left seem to regard as promising. "Today," he writes, "many people are looking for new political approaches that are community-based, value-centered and solution-oriented."[32] It is difficult to know precisely how to understand Wallis at this point. If one takes his language at face value, his formula comes right from the conservative play book. It is not liberals who have been talking about values or about shifting attention away from big government to local, voluntary, community-based organizations.[33]

Wallis admits that "The government is frequently attacked these days—political power has become too concentrated, centralized, intrusive, and unaccountable, especially at the federal level. The large and distant bureaucracies that have come to represent the essence of government are met with disdain by growing numbers of people. Government inefficiency, waste, corruption, and arrogance are all cited, often with good, reason in my opinion."[34] But neither congressional liberals nor the Sojourners organization had ever taken any initiative to expose or criticize such actions while the Democrats controlled Congress.

> From a biblical point of view, there is great reason to suspect and scrutinize concentrations of power—not just politically but theologically. Human nature being what it is, the biblical prophets constantly warned against such concentrations of power and were especially hard on "the king," who embodied political power in biblical times. The powerful are always a threat to the powerless, according to the Bible.[35]

Can Wallis point to anything liberal Democrats have done to break up concentrations of statist power? Even Wallis admits that "The Democrats may [sic] indeed be too protective of big government bureaucracies that provide much of their support."[36]

Given Wallis's past deeds and declarations, can one find a hypothesis that explains this new, anti-governmental rhetoric? Hypothesis One: Wallis has rejected, abandoned, or forgotten his radical past. But there is no evidence of any change of heart, any act of repentance, any lapse of memory about Wallis's past. Besides, his other recent writings show that he remains the same old radical he has always been. Hypothesis Two: Wallis is disingenuous, the kind of man the Scriptures describe as full of guile. Once again, I think not. Hypothesis Three: Wallis is a person who excels in combining bad information with bad judgment. Here, I think, we may be getting close.

There is one other hypothesis to explain Wallis's apparent use of conservative rhetoric at the same time he misrepresents and assaults conservative beliefs. This hypothesis comes from a friend who, like Wallis, was part of the New Left movement in the sixties. He suggests that Wallis's words do not have the same meaning they would have for either a liberal or conservative. Instead, we should read Wallis through the spectacles of New Left ideology. Wallis's prose reminds my friend of language the New Left borrowed from a radical named Saul Alinsky. Because the New Left's anarchistic version of socialism led it to oppose big government, its real enemies have always been big government liberals. Understood in this way, Wallis's rhetoric about abandoning big government could be a revival of the anarcho-socialism he promoted during his pre-seminary days.

Perhaps the day will come when Wallis will confess which of his New Left views are still operative in his thinking. In the meantime, we cannot ignore the possibility that even when Campolo, Sider, and Wallis use similar language, Wallis may be pursuing a different agenda.

CONCLUSION

Many movements that start out as radical tend to become more moderate with the passing of time. This has not been true of Wallis and his movement. The only thing that some people have seen weakening over the years has been his magazine's commitment to evangelical theology. *Sojourners* has seemed more interested in collective guilt resulting from what it sees as American-capitalist oppression of the poor and in a "salvation" of the oppressed from social evils such as racism, sexism, militarism, and homophobia.

Richard John Neuhaus, a former representative of the political Left, warns that *Sojourners* "represents a politically extreme, profoundly self-righteous, and virulently anti-intellectual version of [what Jim Wallis calls] 'biblical politics.'"[37]

If it were not for the serious questions we have noted about Wallis's past, religious conservatives might be more enthusiastic about recent changes in the public discourse of the evangelical Left.

When the evangelical Left continues to treat Jim Wallis as a responsible partner, they do themselves and their cause a disservice. Wallis's past makes it clear that any group of which he is an essential part is not centrist or moderate. Neuhaus has described *Sojourners* as "an echo of every predictable kind of far left, mainly pacifist far left, mishmash of conventional leftisms, presumptuously entertaining—and indeed proclaiming—the conceit that they are prophetic, and I find that pathetic. But it is worse than pathetic because it contains an element of blasphemy."[38]

Neuhaus has gone so far as to question Wallis's claim that his publication is truly evangelical. As K. L. Billingsley observes, "Wallis' theological heroes, after all, are not evangelicals like Dwight Moody and Billy Graham, but [left-wing] Catholic activists such as Dorothy Day and Daniel Berrigan and liberal Protestants such as William Stringfellow."[39]

Billingsley ends his investigative report on Wallis with these words:

> And so it goes, in the wilderness, a voice crying through a bullhorn. This 25-year record of intellectual fecklessness and truckling to tyrannies around the globe should disqualify Jim Wallis from wearing the saint's mantle.... And so the Long March through the Institutions continues, in its latest incarnation, with no rear-view mirror. The people cry for the bread of true spirituality and the self-ordained chaplains of the Left offer the stone soup of their destructive and discredited politics. But something has changed since Jim Wallis got started in the Sixties. The vanguard is now the rear guard. They are still marching, but they are way out of step.[40]

Chapter Seven

Rich Christians and Ron Sider

Ronald J. Sider, professor of theology at Eastern Baptist Theological Seminary in Philadelphia, has been involved, often as an organizer and driving force, in many evangelical Left causes and events. This chapter will evaluate this involvement in three parts: a brief historical outline of the major stages in Sider's rise to prominence; a look at his extraordinarily influential book *Rich Christians in an Age of Hunger* and a review of some of the ways Sider's mind has changed since the first edition of the book appeared in 1977; and a study of Sider's nuclear pacifism.

RONALD SIDER'S RISE TO PROMINENCE

Nine events mark Ron Sider's rise to prominence in the religious Left as well as within the larger evangelical movement. Some of these topics receive more attention in later sections of this chapter or in chapter 8.

1. Evangelicals for McGovern, 1972

The Demoractic party's nomination of George McGovern as its presidential candidate in 1972 signaled a major shift in the party's constituency and ideas. Today, of course, McGovern's ideas rule the party and have, to a large extent, been enacted into law. During the 1960s, politically liberal evangelicals supported Democrats such as

Lyndon Johnson and Hubert Humphrey and were generally happy that the liberal welfare state continued to expand with such rapidity. This to them was a sign of America's growing social conscience. They had little or no understanding what the real consequences of the Great Society programs would be.

When Ron Sider and others started the Evangelicals for McGovern organization, it signaled a new and more radical phase in the development of the evangelical Left. Ralph Reed comments on the long-term significance of McGovern's run for the presidency:

> McGovern became a useful if flawed vehicle for a generation of protest. He turned his campaign over to a youthful army of grassroots guerillas who trooped through the primaries sporting scruffy beards, long hair, tie-dye shirts, and blue jeans.... The McGovern campaign was to the Democratic party what the Goldwater campaign in 1964 was to the Republican party. Despite short-term defeat, it allowed the New Left to take control of the national Democratic party, in whose hands its presidential nominating process remains today. Bill Clinton was present at that creation, and his own ascension to the presidency two decades later represented the coming-of-age of a generation of political rebels.[1]

Even though McGovern was defeated in 1972, the reverence evangelical Leftists still feel for him continues.

2. *The Chicago Declaration, 1973*

The first public gathering of many of the people who would come to represent the evangelical Left occured when fifty evangelicals met in Chicago in 1973 and issued a platform and accompanying paper called *The Chicago Declaration of Social Concern*.[2] Sider helped to organize the conference and edited the book containing both the Declaration and a set of accompanying essays. The Declaration and the book contained much talk about compassion and justice for the poor, although all the key words were left undefined.

A few of the signers such as Carl F. H. Henry and Frank E. Gaebelein were definitely not leftists and decided to sign the document for reasons that have often been misunderstood or misrepresented. Henry had been invited to participate in the conference because evangelical liberals mistakenly saw his 1947 book, *The Uneasy Conscience of Modern Fundamentalism*,[3] as the first conservative move in their direction. Henry's book was certainly a prophetic call for theologically conservative Protestants to face head-on such social issues as racism, justice, and poverty. He criticized evangelicals who neglected the social dimensions of the Gospel, a concern shared by this author and every politically conservative evangelical he knows. But Henry has been critical of the direction many of the signers of the *Chicago Declaration* took in the years following its release. He reports that he and Gabelein

> were disturbed when we received the list of invitees to the 1973 conference which seemed to guarantee in advance something tilted toward Sider's quasi-Marxist emphases. We attended in the hope of preserving some balance; what emerged would have been more objectionable but for the participation of a few of us. We did not sense that Sider was shaping a movement he would vocalize as representative of a large evangelical wing. Of course now that Marxism has been discredited Sider is considerably more discreet.[4]

Carl Henry has consistently distanced himself from the beliefs, practices, and attitudes of the evangelical leftists who ran the Chicago conference and their successors.

3. The Founding of Evangelicals for Social Action (ESA), 1974

For more than twenty years, Evangelicals for Social Action has raised money, held conferences, formed chapters around the nation (many on evangelical college and seminary campuses), and regularly published material expressing the views of Sider and his followers.[5] However, the membership of ESA remains a rather modest 3,200 people.

4. *Rich Christians in an Age of Hunger,* 1977

Ron Sider's book *Rich Christians in an Age of Hunger,* published by InterVarsity Press in 1977, became the manifesto of the evangelical Left. One explanation for the book's success was the fact that liberal faculty members throughout the evangelical academic world made the work required reading in their courses. Tens of thousands of students in Christian colleges got their first exposure to the ideas of the evangelical Left in courses where politically liberal professors expounded Sider's theories. Many of those students have since assumed positions of leadership throughout the church.

Several years ago, one evangelical college president stated publicly that he would not hire any faculty for his school who were not in sympathy with Sider's book and organization. While students at the college report that this president may have abandoned this policy, his statement nonetheless reveals much about the continuing influence of Sider's views.

5. Sider's Nuclear Pacifism, 1982

In 1982, InterVarsity Press published *Nuclear Holocaust and Christian Hope,* co-authored by Sider and Richard K. Taylor. The book was the first major attempt to influence the wider evangelical movement into supporting a position called nuclear pacifism. This was the belief that there could never be justification for any war (even a just war in which a nonaggressor nation sought to defend itself) involving the use of nuclear weapons. It is important to remember that Sider's Anabaptist convictions meant he was a pacifist with respect to all war, even wars where the possible use of nuclear weapons was not a threat. But Sider downplayed his more fundamental pacifism in order to persuade more people to adopt his position on nuclear weapons. A number of evangelical leaders, including Billy Graham, expressed publicly their acceptance of nuclear pacifism.

There was at least one disconcerting implication of Sider's position. If enemy nations possess nuclear weapons and we destroy ours or announce our refusal to use them under any circumstances, any form of military resistance using conventional weapons would be an act of suicide. A commitment to nuclear pacifism would have to be followed by more than unilateral disarmament; the inevitable consequence would be unconditional surrender.

6. Sider's "Completely Pro-Life" Position, 1987

In 1987, Sider published *Completely Pro-Life*, a book detailing a new kind of pro-life position.[6] Many evangelical liberals who became pro-life did so under Sider's influence. During the 1980s, Sider conceived of a theory that he believed held the promise of providing common ground for the values of political liberals and the concerns of pro-life Christians. It proved to be a strategically clever move that gave Sider a way to influence evangelical and Roman Catholic pro-life supporters into accepting the rest of his liberal political agenda.

7. *JustLife* Magazines, 1988–1992

In 1988 Sider published the first of several polished-looking magazines, titled *JustLife*, that contained articles on the consistently pro-life position by well-known evangelical and Roman Catholic religious leaders. He published new versions in 1990 and 1992. The publication also contained a political scorecard to enable readers to grade various members of the U.S. Congress according to Sider's *JustLife* criteria. It looked as though Sider's purpose was to help approved political candidates receive as many evangelical and Catholic votes as possible. Whenever we hear evangelical Leftists like Jim Wallis, Tony Campolo, and Tom Sine deride what they describe as the Religious Right's efforts to influence elections and legislation, it is important to remember that the Religious Left was doing this long before the Christian Coalition came along.

8. Declaration II, 1993

In 1993 many of the same evangelical liberals met once again in Chicago for a sort of twentieth anniversary of the original

Chicago Declaration. This time, centrists such as Carl Henry were noticeably absent. Ron Sider, Tony Campolo, Jim Wallis, and Tom Sine were present, along with well-known author Richard Foster; David McKenna, president of Asbury Theological Seminary; and Jay Kesler, president of Taylor University.

Mary Fisher, a professor at Asbury Theological Seminary, presented a paper with the rather cumbersome title "Spirituality as Counter-Culture: The Power of the Spirit, and Gender, Race, Class and the Status Quo." Catherine Clark Kroeger, president of Christians for Biblical Equality,[7] read a paper titled "Sex and the Saints: Ancient Sexual Attitudes and the New Testament Response." Jim Wallis read a paper titled "The People Perish: The Need for a New Social Vision in America." Perhaps he meant that America had failed to grasp his *old* vision.

It was apparent from these presentations that the evangelical Left's agenda had moved far beyond the original concerns of the first *Chicago Declaration* and was now keeping pace with the liberal interests of the nineties. Outside of the usual participants in the secular and religious Left, no one seemed to pay much attention to the second Chicago conference. No doubt, the disappointing results of that conference were one reason for the attempt two years later to garner new attention with the document called *The Cry for Renewal.*

9. *The Cry for Renewal,* 1995

The release of *The Cry for Renewal* in 1995 seems to have attracted more attention for the evangelical Left than any event in its recent past. At least, this is the view of people like Jim Wallis. Because of the importance of this document to the evangelical Left cause, it will be the subject of a later chapter in this book.

A CLOSER LOOK AT *RICH CHRISTIANS IN AN AGE OF HUNGER*

There are numerous points in Sider's book *Rich Christians in an Age of Hunger* that informed religious conservatives can accept. When

Sider advises Christians to live simpler lives, spend less of their disposable income on themselves, and use a larger share for advancing God's kingdom and easing suffering in the world, his suggestions may have merit. Proposals like these call for voluntary action instead of reliance on the coercive activity of a large and oppressive government. Of course, there are times when even some of these suggestions appear designed more to assuage liberal guilt than to accomplish anything substantive. Sider's best proposals tend to show up more frequently in the third and latest edition of his book, in which his understanding of capitalism is more adequate.

Informed conservatives, therefore, need not oppose Sider's calls for voluntary action. Protests should be expected, however, whenever Sider starts implying that the federal government is doing God's work when it uses its coercive powers, somewhat like a contemporary Robin Hood, and takes from some to give to others. One wishes that the Ron Sider of 1977 knew what the Ron Sider of 1995 has finally come to recognize, namely, that the huge, liberal welfare state has done far more harm than good to the poor, while accumulating a national debt of five trillion dollars ($5,000,000,000,000) doing it.

Errors in Early Editions of *Rich Christians*

The first edition of Sider's book contained numerous examples of what happens when social activists proceed in ignorance of the accepted tools of economic analysis. More often than not, they turn bad situations into something far worse.[8] For example, Sider suggested that Americans should unilaterally begin to pay more than a market price for certain commodities from poor countries. He seemed unaware of the long-range consequences such policies would have on the economy of poorer nations. But Sider's economic blunder did not escape the attention of George Mavrodes, a University of Michigan philosopher:

> Sider usually seems unaware that his policies may have different results than he intends. Suppose that we [Americans]

voluntarily increased the price that we pay for crude rubber (a recurrent suggestion of Sider's), then, Sider says, rubber workers would get higher wages. Fine. But wouldn't rubber producers scramble to increase production? And wouldn't land and labor be diverted from other enterprises, such as food production, to cash in on higher rubber prices? Since we don't need more rubber, the increased production would represent a waste of resources. Sider seems not to notice such consequences.[9]

Robert Frykenberg, a historian at the University of Wisconsin, pointed out that it is easy for writers like Sider to announce that the world's poor need food and help. Sider stops short, however, of the much more difficult task of describing some effective and realistic way of meeting those needs:

> But without showing us exactly how the world's hungry are to be fed, nothing results except the mouthing of pious platitudes and highly emotional exhortations to act. Such well-meaning efforts to help are at best inefficient and wasteful, and, at worst, utterly self-defeating and demoralizing. Often, like the children's crusades, they end up doing more harm than good.[10]

The first edition of Sider's book typified the evangelical Left's approach toward social problems. While their sincere compassion was often wedded to a political and economic ideology that may have reflected all the proper emotions, their economic competence deserved a failing grade. The emotional side of evangelical social concern—loving and caring—is only half the struggle. The best intentions cannot aid the poor unless they are channeled into actions that are informed by sound economic theory and practice. When "aid" is grounded on bad economics, it will usually make any bad situation worse.

"Is God a Marxist?"

The 1995 edition of Ron Sider's book includes a denial that he has ever been a Marxist or a socialist,[11] even though many readers thought he was. Pages 72–77 in the first edition make problematic his current claim that he was never a Marxist. Sider headed this material with the question, "Is God a Marxist?" The five pages that follow purport to offer extensive biblical support for a coercive govermental redistribution of wealth. Sider's failure to provide a negative answer to his question suggests that he did think God was a Marxist.

The Jubilee Principle

Possibly the biggest blunder in Sider's first edition was also the section that led many of his readers to believe that the Bible endorses socialism. The passage, entitled "The Jubilee Principle," appears on pages 90–92.

The Bible's account of the Jubilee Year is given in Leviticus 25. Read superficially—*very* superficially—it is easy to understand why the Religious Left eagerly embraced this text. Almost every prominent member of the evangelical Left has at one time or another appealed to Leviticus 25 in support of the redistributionist notion of "justice."[12] The basic idea behind redistributionist "justice" is that the state must seek an equality of people's holdings by forcibly taking from some people and giving to others. In the process, of course, the employees of the state hold back enough to pay their own substantial salaries, benefits, and retirement packages.

Leviticus 25 announces that every fiftieth year in Israel would be a year of Jubilee. As the evangelical Left read the passage, anyone to whom bad things had happened in the previous forty-nine years would be delivered from their misfortune at the Jubilee. Poor families that had had to sell their land would receive the land back free of charge. Slaves would be delivered from their chains. To quote Sider's account of the Jubilee,

> Leviticus 25 is one of the most radical texts in all of Scripture. At least it seems that way for people born in countries committed to either laissez-faire economics[13] or commu-

nism. Every fifty years, God said, all land was to return to the original owners—without compensation! Physical handicaps, death of a breadwinner or lack of natural ability may lead some people to become poorer than others. But God does not want such disadvantages to lead to greater and greater divergence of wealth and poverty. God therefore gave his people a law which would equalize land ownership every fifty years (Lev. 25:10–24).[14]

These words were repeated verbatim in the second edition of *Rich Christians,* published in 1984.[15] Sider was still using this kind of rhetoric in late 1988.[16] In retrospect, it appears the evangelical Left was so anxious to find biblical support for the Christian socialism they endorsed that they failed in exegesis. As E. Calvin Beisner describes this situation, "A more thorough case of reading into a text what one hopes to find can hardly exist."[17]

Sider's claim that *all* land was returned to the original owners without compensation contained several errors. For one thing, a careful reading of Leviticus 25 reveals that some forms of wealth were not affected by the Jubilee principle. For example, sold land located within walled cities could be redeemed within one year. Once that time had passed, the exchange was regarded as permanent and immune to the changes otherwise affected by the Jubilee (Lev. 25:29–30). Other forms of income (what economists call "capital," as in *capitalism)* such as fishing boats were also excluded from the Jubilee practice. It is also true that the Jubilee did not benefit all the poor. It did not, for example, help immigrants who had no original inheritance. Moreover, given the relatively short lifespan of people in those days, the fifty-year interval between Jubilees made it inevitable that many people would not live long enough to see a Jubilee Year. Obviously, such people would never be helped at all.

Furthermore, if the Jubilee had been instituted,[18] it would have terminated the buying and selling of land as we know it in favor of leases made more or less valuable by the number of years remaining until the next Jubilee. Under such conditions, anyone contemplating the acquisition of land would know that he was only buying the use of the land for a certain number of years. Land would then be most valuable in the first years immediately following a Jubilee, but would be worth relatively little in the years just before a new Jubilee. Instead of land outside of walled cities being bought and sold, it is more accurate to say that such land could only be rented or leased and that all such leases would end with the arrival of the Jubilee.

Read correctly, Leviticus 25 endorses a number of policies that look more like capitalism than socialism.

Sometime after 1988, Sider finally saw the light. Speaking at Wheaton College in 1995, Sider admitted there were errors in his handling of Leviticus 25 in his book. He said that "Leviticus 25 makes clear that the new owner[19] pays for the number of crops between the purchase date and the time of the next Jubilee. The longer the time till that next Jubilee, the higher the price. The purchaser[20] really acquires the right to the intervening crops, but not to unlimited, unending ownership. Therefore to speak of the land returning to the original owner 'without compensation' becomes confusing."

Sider's willingness to admit his earlier mistakes makes him unique among members of the evangelical Left. While it is comforting to know that Sider admitted this and other errors to the students and faculty of Wheaton College, it is puzzling why he did not also report that his new positions have been influenced by evangelical conservatives.

Was Sider a Socialist?

In his address at Wheaton College in 1995, Sider denied that he is a socialist or that he was one when he wrote the first edition of *Rich Christians*. While I take him at his word, I am persuaded that Sider still lacks a clear understanding of the true nature of either socialism or capitalism. When Sider talks about socialism today, he means "a centrally planned economy where the government owns most of the means of production."[21]

While an economy like this would certainly be socialist, Sider fails to recognize that most of the world's economies reflect degrees of governmental control and coercion that stop short of public ownership of factories, railroads, airlines, and the like. Hitler's name for his form of facism was *National Socialism*. While the Nazis permitted significant amounts of private ownership of the means of production, their economy was socialist because of the various forms of statist control still present in their system. Economic systems that I describe later in this book as interventionist are often just slightly watered-down versions of socialism. The fact that Sider fails to acknowledge this is understandable, because the kind of economic system he now prefers is best understood, not as capitalism but as the diluted version of socialism I describe later under the name "interventionism."

Is Sider Now a Capitalist?

In his Wheaton address, Sider said, "I would not be as critical of capitalism [today] as in the first edition.[22] Today, I would argue that the market economy is a better framework for the economic order than any alternative we know. I did not say that clearly in the first edition. I do today."[23] But Sider follows this admission with some remarkable verbal zigzagging.

Zig: Sider waffles by suggesting that many contemporary situations still require massive statist intervention with people's holdings.[24] *Zag:* He waffles again by adding, "None of these points lead me to conclude that we ought to prefer socialism, even democratic socialism. I think the market framework is preferable. Therefore, I favor and work for a democratic political order and a market economy as the best political-economic framework currently available."[25]

Zig: Sider then seems to retract his words as he urges Christian voters to elect liberal politicians whose voting records reveal opposition to the market system. "I conclude," he writes, that some government intervention in the economy is warranted."[26] Unfortunately, this only shows that Sider still does not understand the true nature of a market economy, something I will explain more fully in a later chapter. *Zag:* In his final act of indecisiveness, Sider declares, "I am more cautious and suspicious about government intervention today than earlier. With disturbing frequency, government bureaucracies and regulations mess things up more than they make things better. So I would require more specific data today before vigorously favoring government intervention."[27]

If Sider is a capitalist, he is one only in a very loose sense of the word, a sense that is still consistent with the kinds of governmental interference that has characterized political liberalism in America. Nevertheless, if he had acknowledged even these modest concessions to "capitalism" in the first edition of *Rich Christians*, the significant split between evangelical conservatives and liberals might never have grown as large as it has. For one thing, the Jim Wallis of 1977 would have isolated himself from the kinds of positions Sider now defends.

Sider on Wealth

Members of the evangelical Left often reflect a hostile attitude toward people who have been financially successful in life, a fact that may result in part from a failure to understand the role of entrepreneurship and risk-taking and in part from living a sheltered life in academia as beneficiaries of the largesse of others. This attitude is apparent in the first two editions of Sider's book. It is one thing to criticize people whose wealth results from unjust conduct, such as politicians who use their high office and power to enrich themselves.[28] But whence comes the hostility of leftists to people who succeed honorably and in the process create jobs and opportunities for other people?

I once shared a platform with Sider where he actually said that the Bible condemns all wealth. I challenged this claim by pointing out that all of the biblical indictments of wealth he quoted that day concerned wealth that had been acquired unjustly. Claims that the Bible condemns wealth or that God hates all the rich are clearly incompatible with the teachings of Jesus. While

Jesus certainly condemned materialism and the compulsive quest for wealth, he did not teach that being rich necessarily means being evil.[29] Jesus did not see anything sinful in the ownership of houses, clothes, and other economic goods. He had wealthy friends and followers (Luke 14:1); he stayed in the homes of wealthy people; he ate at their tables (Luke 11:37).

A number of Jesus' parables provide insights into his views on wealth. In Luke 16:9 and the accompanying parable, Jesus taught that his followers should use their resources with the same dedication and keen judgment as the unjust steward. In the parable of the rich farmer (Luke 12:16–21), Jesus did not condemn the farmer for making money but rather for his single-minded concern with his own wealth and happiness. The man was a fool because he was a self-centered materialist who had forgotten God; he was not a fool because he had been a successful businessman. The parable of Lazarus and the rich man (Luke 16:19–31) does not teach that a person's eternal destiny is determined by the amount of possessions he acquires in this life. It is implied that Lazarus was a believer. It is clear that the rich man went to hell because of a godless and self-centered life, a fact made evident by the way he used his wealth and by his indifference to the poor.

Jesus' teaching stresses human obligations that cannot be fulfilled unless one first has certain financial resources. For example, passages that oblige believers to use their resources for God's purposes presuppose the legitimacy of private ownership.[30] Jesus taught that children have an obligation to care for their parents (Matt. 15:3–9) and that his followers ought to be generous in their support of worthy causes (Matt. 6:2–4). It is rather difficult to fulfill such obligations unless one has certain financial resources.

Jesus often spoke about wealth without condemning it (Matt.13:44–46; 21:33–46). He praised those who through wise management and careful stewardship created wealth. When he did call on people to renounce their possessions, his statements reflected special conditions; in one instance, for example, he made this demand in a situation where people had made their possessions into a god (Luke 18:22–24). Instead of condemning wealth, then, Jesus' teaching offers an important perspective on how people living in materialistic surroundings should view the material world. What Jesus condemned was not wealth per se but the improper acquisition and use of wealth.

All Christians, rich or poor, need to recognize that whatever they possess is theirs *temporarily* as stewards under God. Wealth that is accumulated dishonestly or that becomes a controlling principle in life falls under God's judgment. Wealth resulting from honest labor and wise investment, handled by people who recognize their role as stewards under God, does not.

Those who draw attention only to passages in which Jesus indicted prosperous people are presenting only part of his teaching. We must avoid the temptation of selecting a few passages from the Gospels that reflect our preferred opinions and lifestyle. Jesus' teaching about money, wealth, and poverty is extremely diverse.

A CLOSER LOOK AT SIDER'S VIEWS OF DISARMAMENT

Another weakness of the Religious Left that many would like forgotten, at least for the moment, was the zealous calling on the United States to disarm itself of nuclear weapons unilaterally without regard for reciprocal acts of the part of the Soviet Union. Ronald Sider was an outspoken advocate of this view in the 1980s, and he has not subsequently published any statements to the contrary.

In the book *Nuclear Holocaust and Christian Hope,* published in 1982, Sider and co-author Richard K. Taylor set forth a view that they called Nuclear Pacifism.[31] As Keith and Karl Payne explain, "The usual approach of antinuclear groups, even some Christian groups, is to shock people with mind-numbing descriptions of nuclear war, and then argue that because the results would be so completely destructive the U.S. must disarm—even if the Soviet Union does not."[32] This was the strategy adopted by Sider and Taylor; even the possession of nuclear weapons is immoral.

Sider fully understood that such action would be followed by an occupation of the United States by the Red Army and such allies as Cuba and East Germany. Sider's recommendation to

Christians during such an occupation was passive resistance along the lines of Gandhi, using the example of peace-loving Christians placing flowers in the gun barrels of the occupying soldiers. Left unstated in Sider's appeal was the reason that Gandhi's passive resistance eventually succeeded. Gandhi, after all, was resisting a civilized power (Great Britain) publicly committed to the rule of law and sensitive to censure from other nations, should Britain act brutally. What would have been Gandhi's fate had he been resisting powers such as Hitler's Germany or Stalin's Soviet Union?

K. L. Billingsley said of the Sider-Taylor book that it might "very well be the world's longest suicide note, suicide being the sure outcome of his nonmilitary defense plan."[33] It apparently did not occur to Sider and other members of the Religious Left that a policy they recommended because it would supposedly lessen tension and danger in the world would result instead in enormous injustice and loss of life. As Keith and Karl Payne have argued, unilateral disarmanent is immoral and ineffective. It is immoral "because it would place the safety and security of all Americans in the hands of a hostile and aggressive power."[34] It is ineffective because it would jeopardize the safety and security of our neighbors and alies. While allowing nonresistance as a pacifist choice in the face of attack, the Paynes contend that Christian pacifists "have no biblical right or justification to require others to die with them because of their own personal choice." Christians should beware, they continue, "of those shouting 'peace, peace,' while leading the United States down a path to conquest and repression."[35]

Now that the peoples of Russia, the Ukraine, and other former republics of the Soviet Union have, at least temporarily, repudiated the Communist system, one might reflect on how different the world would be today if the United States had followed the advice of the Religious Left. One thing is clear: The collapse of communism, the liberation of Eastern Europe, and the breakup of the Soviet Union would never have occurred. The Communist dictatorships of the world would have been too busy enjoying their occupation of what once was the free world.

IS RON SIDER A LIBERAL?

Like Jim Wallis, Ron Sider today wants people to believe he is a centrist instead of a liberal. But is he? One of Sider's own friends will help us answer this question.

In a 1992 *Christianity Today* article treating Sider as one of the heroes of the contemporary evangelical movement, staff writer Tim Stafford describes Sider's politics as "main-stream Democratic party, except for conservative stances on homosexuality and abortion."[36] Stafford does not identify Sider as a centrist. More telling, perhaps, is the answer Stafford received when he asked Tony Campolo if Sider is a liberal. In Campolo's words, "If you want to know [Sider's] view on capital punishment, you don't even have to ask. If you want to know his view on El Salvador, you don't have to ask. If you want to know what he thinks about disarmament and the military, you don't even have to ask. If it looks liberal, and it smells liberal, and it tastes liberal, it's liberal."[37] And so we learn, just a couple of short years ago, before the evangelical Left hit upon the strategy of portraying themselves as centrists, that even Tony Campolo regarded his good friend Ron Sider as the quintessential liberal.

Chapter Eight

Sider on Peace, Justice, and Life

M ost evangelical Christians agree that killing an unborn baby as a form of birth control or gender selection or simply because it is unwanted is immoral.[1] Evangelicals who are not pro-life are typically allies of the evangelical Left.[2]

SIDER ON BEING COMPLETELY PRO-LIFE

For a number of years Ronald Sider has been a strong supporter of the pro-life position among people usually identified within the evangelical Left. Pro-life Christians are in debt to Sider for what he has done to bring many in the evangelical Left to a pro-life stance.

During the 1980s, Sider and others who followed him began to urge pro-life Christians to adopt a "consistently pro-life" position.[3] While persons who represent this view oppose abortion (in almost all cases), they want Christians who say they support life to be consistent and apply their pro-life stance to several related issues. Their extensive agenda includes opposition to capital punishment and nuclear weapons, "economic injustice," environmental pollution, and substance abuse, including tobacco.

Sider's Defense of the Unborn

Ron Sider is surely correct when he argues that the problem of abortion results from "a secular individualism that makes the self-

interest of the individual the highest value. By their sexual irrespon-
sibility and failure to share fairly in the burdens of child care and par-
enting, many men have placed their individual selfish concerns
above the rights of children, women and the larger community."[4]

What we find in the defense of abortion by secular feminists is
"the same destructive, individualistic selfishness," set in a context in
which they appeal to the "very individualism which has long led
many men to trample on the needs of children and the larger community. The solution surely is for both men and women to abandon
secular individualism and refuse to place self above all others."[5]

While it is clear that Sider is on the side of the unborn, it is
less clear whether he understands how his efforts to combat other
social problems as an extension of the pro-life position effectively
undermines the pro-life cause.

The "Consistently Pro-Life" Movement

As appreciative as pro-life supporters may be of Sider's defense
of the unborn, his efforts have not been without controversy. With
each passing year, his representation of the pro-life cause has
become increasingly mixed with his larger agenda. Since the
appearance in 1987 of *Completely Pro-Life,* a book he edited, Sider
has worked hard to form a coalition of pro-life Protestants and
Catholics who otherwise support liberal social programs. Sider has
also sought to harness support from left-wing opponents of America's efforts to defend itself militarily against nuclear and terrorist
attacks from other nations and organizations.

The "consistently pro-life" movement, as it is sometimes
called, gets much of its energy from opposing what many have
referred to as America's "killing fields": the hospitals and abortion
clinics where one-and-a-half million lives are snuffed out each
year. Sider's movement then channels that energy and moral fer-
vor into support for traditional liberal social and political causes.
If you are really pro-life, Sider argues, then you will act on behalf
of other life-related issues. These other issues are closely aligned
with the concerns of the political Left.

Basic to Sider's movement is the claim that abortion is only one way in which a pro-life stance is challenged. The majority of the pro-life movement are criticized for their supposed inconsistency. Why, Sider's followers ask, do other pro-life supporters ignore the threats that cigarettes, drugs, nuclear weapons, and capital punishment pose to life? In the same way, he then turns to his allies on the left and asks, "Why do so many liberal and radical activists champion nuclear disarmament to protect the sanctity of human life and then defend the destruction of one-and-a-half million unborn babies each year? Are 'sexual freedom' and affluent lifestyles finally more important than helpless, inconvenient babies?"[6]

By this means, Sider presents himself as somewhere in the middle of America's social and political strife. While he agrees with the left's stand on disarmament and social issues, he criticizes their inconsistency when they fail to extend humanitarian concern to the unborn. Sider applauds the commitment of the right to defending the unborn, but criticizes their refusal to extend their concern for life to what he thinks are equally important pro-life positions.

Several months before the 1988 presidential election, Sider's movement published a thirty-two-page magazine titled *JustLife/88*. The magazine included articles by evangelist Billy Graham, Joseph Cardinal Bernardin of Chicago, and Roberta Hestenes, the president of Eastern College, among other authors. Also included were advertisements for the latest books on liberal political issues and invitations to join Evangelicals for Social Action and a left-wing Roman Catholic organization called Pax Christi.

JustLife/88 stressed that the consistently pro-life movement regards justice as a "seamless garment." Once the various segments of the consistently pro-life agenda have been identified, the magazine proposed, they are inseparable. The catch was that, with the exception of opposition to abortion, the magazine's agenda was essentially indistinguishable from well-known liberal objectives.

JustLife/88 argued for a "wholistic vision" of things, calling on pro-life Americans to evaluate the votes of members of Congress in terms of their fidelity to three major groups of issues: abortion, the nuclear arms race, and what was ambiguously referred to as "economic justice." A number of other issues—also part of the seamless garment—were present in the background: capital punishment, the environment, racism, and sexism.

Readers also found a scorecard with numbers showing how well members of Congress had supported fifteen issues identified by the magazine's editors as reflective of consistently pro-life convictions. Five Senate votes were used to assess economic justice; the amendments, all sponsored by liberal Democrats, concerned the allocation of funds for a variety of social programs and the withholding of money from the Strategic Defense Initiative, the Nicaraguan contras, and other defense issues. According to the magazine, a senator who voted with the liberal Democrats on these issues was consistently pro-life.

Another group of five votes reflected a senator's convictions on the nuclear arms race adjudged by liberal criteria.

A separate group of five votes dealt with abortion. But at this point, an embarrassing irony appeared. Most of the Senate liberals, whose votes on economic justice and nuclear disarmament had pleased the magazine's editors, voted *in favor of abortion;* they voted *against life.* Because liberal senators like Edward Kennedy, Howard Metzenbaum, and Alan Cranston voted for the ten liberal positions on economic justice and disarmament, they were assured of a score of 67 percent, even though they voted against all of the recommended curbs on abortion. However, conservative senators who voted the way the magazine's editors preferred on the abortion issue but not on the ten liberal issues would score just 33 percent.

Through this tally, *JustLife/88* effectively advised Christians to vote for the most pro-abortion members of the U.S. Senate. It also created the impression that Christians should vote against politically conservative senators, even though they were the Senate's most consistent opponents of abortion.

A similar inconsistency appeared in the magazine's scorecard for members of the U.S. House. As Richard John Neuhaus observed,

In the House of Representatives, denizens of the leftmost ideological fever swamps and relentless champions of abortion (e.g., Ron Dellums of California, George Crockett of Michigan, and Ted Weiss of New York) get generally favorable grades. The highly prejudiced scorecard rates Congressman Henry Hyde of Illinois as an opponent of life 60% of the time.[7]

Neuhaus said further, "The entire logic of the election guide is that a candidate's vote for government day care, for example, cancels out his vote against protecting the unborn."[8] The consequence of Sider's publication was simply this, according to Neuhaus: *If the candidates favored by JustLife are elected, it will guarantee an overwhelming pro-abortion majority in the United States Congress.* Obviously, there are many people who would welcome that."[9] Nevertheless, many of these pro-abortion people would be considered allies of the "consistently pro-life" position.

(About a month before the presidential election of 1988, I asked Sider personally whether he was going to vote for George Bush or for Michael Dukakis, who stood on opposite sides of the abortion issue. Sider said he would vote for Dukakis. When I countered that this information contradicted Sider's pro-life position, he responded with the claim that Reagan and Bush were responsible for the deaths of millions of babies every year because of their failure to do enough about malnutrition and disease around the world. Yet, the likelihood of *any* American president's finding ways to alter the tragic conditions in Third World nations in one year or even four years approaches statistical impossibility.)[10]

Neuhaus argued that Sider's badly arranged scorecard required an apology from those who perpetrated "the arrogantly wrongheaded fiasco that is JustLife."[11] The very structure of the JustLife project "relativizes, trivializes, and finally neutralizes the question of abortion." Therefore, Neuhaus insisted, we must "look elsewhere for an explanation of why people who say they are profoundly committed to the protection of the unborn endorse a program that, were it successful, would assure the triumph of pro-abortion forces in American political life."[12] When we recall that JustLife equates its own political agenda with the will of God, the result, according to Neuhaus, "is as gross a display of moral arrogance as anything witnessed in recent American history."[13]

The debate over JustLife and the consistently pro-life movement generated enough heat to produce a long exchange in the
July 14, 1989, issue of *Christianity Today*. The task of critiquing
JustLife went to Charles E. White, a professor at an evangelical
college. White pointed to the confusion between ends and means
as one place where he thought the JustLife people went wrong.
Even when the correct ends or goals are pursued, the selection of
the wrong means assures that the goals will remain unreachable.

JustLife was right to say, White argued, "that God's will is
plain in its opposition to abortion, economic injustice, and war.
The elimination of these three wrongs is clearly God's goal for our
society. Saving lives by ending abortion, poverty, and the threat of
nuclear war is certainly an end that God wants us to reach."[14]

The problem, however, was that JustLife "forgets that having
the right end is only part of the answer. The issue is more complex. In the real world of politics, we have to have the correct
means to achieve our good ends. Good intentions are not
enough."[15] Few of us know any Americans who have evil intentions when it comes to things like peace and poverty; everyone
claims to want to help end poverty and promote peace. The question, White insisted, is seldom about ends; it is about the proper
means to those ends.

But in the battle over abortion, the people on opposite sides *are*
promoting opposing goals. Pro-abortion people demand the right
to destroy fetal life; pro-life people seek to save life. Furthermore,
the ambiguities and complexities that make correct decisions in the
social and political arena so difficult do not apply in the matter of
abortion. "God's Word makes it clear that He wants society to protect weak, innocent, and defenseless people," White argued.[16] Biblical passages such as Exodus 21:22–25, Psalm 139:13–16, Proverbs
24:11–12, Jeremiah 1:5, and Luke 1:15 teach that the unborn child
is a human person whose life is valuable in God's eyes.

So when it comes to the issue of abortion, there can be little
doubt where the battle lines are to be drawn or where people who
claim to be Christians should be standing. But the issues of "economic justice" and peace are different in the sense that while sincere

Christians ought to agree about their desirability as ends, we may nonetheless disagree over the best means to achieve those ends. This truth led White to claim that "JustLife is not being biblically faithful when it identifies one particular political position as the God-ordained means to achieve these godly ends. Here it is going beyond the Word of God into areas where God has not authoritatively spoken. It is making conclusions it has reached on its own and passing them off as God's inerrant revelation."[17]

JustLife's confusion over the means-ends issue resulted in political recommendations that were counterproductive, White argued. Its congressional scorecard implied that the votes of pro-abortion liberals like Howard Metzenbaum of Ohio and Alan Cranston of California are twice as pleasing to God as the votes of a pro-life senator like William Armstrong of Colorado (now retired) or a pro-life congressman like Henry Hyde of Illinois.

Obviously stung by some of these criticisms, Sider tried to play down the blatant bias of *JustLife/88* and denied that his movement sides with one particular political position—a claim that people familiar with his organization find disingenuous. Sider did admit that the use of percentages in *JustLife/88* was a minor mistake that some readers misused to reach conclusions that the magazine's editors did not intend. He promised that future issues would avoid the mistakes of the first. With these promises in mind, it is instructive to see what Sider's group did in its next publication, *JustLife/90*.

JustLife/90 appeared prior to the congressional elections of 1990. It included an essay by U.S. Senator Mark Hatfield of Oregon, a long-time supporter of Jim Wallis's Sojourners movement, and articles by several politically liberal Roman Catholics. Once again, its focus was the new scorecard for Senate and House candidates.

The 1990 issue differed from its predecessor in at least two ways. First, percentages were not used as a measurement of congressional votes. Second, the identification of key votes (reduced to four votes each on economic justice, abortion, and nuclear arms) appeared to have been chosen more carefully so as not to reflect quite so badly on politicians like Senator Hatfield, who supported the JustLife organization.[18] Nevertheless, a careful examination of the test votes on economic and nuclear issues reflects the same problems noted in connection with *JustLife/88*. The identified issues were not relevant to the means-end question discussed earlier. In other words, sincere Christians could agree about the important ends of helping the poor or avoiding nuclear conflagration while disagreeing about Sider's liberal, one-sided set of means to achieve those ends.

For example, one vote in the area of "economic justice" hinged on support for the more extreme minimum-wage bill favored by congressional liberals. This ignored strong economic arguments that minimum-wage laws do not help the poor but, in fact, favor the highly paid members of large labor unions. In the long run, these economic experts argue, such laws actually harm the poor by making unskilled workers less employable. As African-American economists Walter Williams and Thomas Sowell argue, minimum-wage legislation tends to do most of its harm to unskilled black workers.[19] It is ironic that Sider and the ESA supported legislation that was potentially anti-poor and anti-black in its effects.

It is worth noting that this issue belongs to a sphere of economics where Sider's thinking has begun to change. Is it possible that some future issue of *JustLife* will use opposition to minimum-wage legislation as the true test of a "consistently pro-life" position?

Another complex issue that *JustLife/90* oversimplified is the matter of military aid to El Salvador. Obviously, there were deplorable human rights abuses by all sides in the Salvadoran conflict, even though listening to the Left, one would think no abuses were ever perpetrated by the Communist rebels. Regrettably, *JustLife/90* took the extreme Left position that undermined any real hope of ending the Marxist insurgency. Ironically, it also had the effect of expanding the power of corrupt government officials and undermined the cause of democracy in El Salvador. But such thinking seems all too typical of the Religious Left. For them, the enemy is never on the left; by definition, it is always on the "right." While the "right" in the Salvadoran conflict must bear its load of guilt, there was plenty of blame to spread around among all the combatants.

Many believe the far Left in the United States either wanted the Marxist rebels in El Salvador to win, thus producing another Nicaragua, or at least wanted them to have significant power in a new government, thus raising the hope of a more gradual Marxist takeover in the future. These claims are disputed by the evangelical Left, of course. But that is precisely the point: Why select this highly controversial vote as a test of congressional morality and honor?

Unfortunately, every one of the *JustLife/90* test votes on economic justice and the nuclear issue was highly controversial and concerned issues on which good and honorable people can disagree. But such legitimate disagreement was ignored by the editors of the magazine, who appear to have set their tests up in ways that best served their own political agenda.

An Uncritical Alliance Between Christians and Politicians?

One additional point about Sider's JustLife experiment deserves mention. The leaders of the evangelical Left have attacked the Christian Coalition and other conservative Christian activists for the uncritical alliance they have created between Christianity and conservative politicians. Liberals today act as though any action of this kind constitutes a betrayal of the Christian faith. But such accusations seem hypocritical in light of the evidence. Jim Wallis, as we have seen, has been an ardent supporter of Christian alliances with far Left political entities. In this chapter we have seen that Ron Sider, the person who comes closest to being a moderate member of the evangelical Left, has himself spent years trying to elect liberal, typically Democratic, candidates to public office. Later on, we will learn about Tony Campolo's long association with the Democratic party and his current status as a close friend of President Clinton.

Summary

As we have shown, one unfortunate result of the consistently pro-life movement is that the cause of the unborn continues to get lost in the shuffle. Recommendations to vote against pro-life candidates and support pro-abortion candidates are not, I suggest, good examples of a consistently pro-life position. To repeat an earlier quote from Richard John Neuhaus, the JustLife project "relativizes, trivializes, and finally neutralizes the question of abortion."[20]

Charles E. White was correct, therefore, when he wrote that "JustLife should stop its talk about a 'consistent ethic of life' and make it clear that there is only one issue facing our government where Americans openly disagree about the ends we are trying to reach: abortion. God's will is clear on the ends and means [in this case], and rejecting God's will in this matter is such a moral monstrosity that it dwarfs all other squabbling about means."[21] What this means, White continued, is, "The people in JustLife should stop trying to divert the concern, energy, and money of committed Christians away from the God-given ends of the prolife movement and into side issues relating to human means. They should give priority to the one issue where there is a clearly defined method of fulfilling God's will, and then, with other Christians, seek his mind about how to do his will in other areas."[22]

It is clear, then, that the seamless garment of the consistently pro-life movement tears apart at a critical seam, compromising support for the cause of the unborn. Christians who are truly and consistently pro-life will not sacrifice the unborn on the altar of politics.

Nor is abortion the only issue on which the evangelical Left appears inconsistent and short-sighted. Let us consider the cause of "peace and justice" as another example.

CHRISTIANS FOR PEACE?

A friend of mine had been at a gathering of evangelicals where the participants had been asked to stand, identify themselves, and name the organization they represented. When the turn came for a member of Evangelicals for Social Action, the person identified his organization and added smugly, "I am a peace-and-justice Christian!" His implication was that he was the *only* Christian in the room working for peace and justice.

The evangelical Left's belief that it has had a monopoly on the vitally important concepts of peace and justice reveals much about the arrogance and sense of moral superiority that, until recently at least, used to characterize it. A careful analysis of the terms "peace" and "justice" will reveal some serious problems in the way the religous left handles these notions.

Consider, for example, the left's distortion of the biblical term *shalom* (peace). The Left has misused *shalom* to justify a form of pacifism that would have allowed countless tyrants—from Hitler and Stalin to present-day totalitarians—the opportunity to impose their ruthless power on helpless people with a free hand.

Moreover, as Dean Curry notes, the religious Left also misuses *shalom* "to legitimate political agendas that are more often than not ideologically leftist."[23] Such actions ignore the fact that there are three types of peace in the Bible. The first is peace with God. The second is peace with oneself. The third is the important matter of achieving peace among human beings. The first two kinds of peace are available only to believers in Christ. In the Bible, the third type is never equated with pacifism. It refers instead to the absence of conflict in the real world and is, more often than not, a consequence of nonaggressor nations' being strong enough to deter aggression against either themselves or weaker nations.

Peace-and-justice Christians also fail to see that the biblical concept of *shalom* contains nuances not found in the English word "peace," such as the ideas of completeness and wholeness. This leads Curry to say that *shalom* "is a gift of God, brought about, not through the work of man's hands, but by God. The peace of *shalom* is an eschatological peace which awaits the consummation of history itself."[24] Hence, biblical *shalom* is not simply the absence of war and cannot be tied in any essential way to pacifism. The Religious Left's pursuit of "peace" on its terms will only make the world a more dangerous place for everyone. Real peace in the real world is the last thing the policies of peace-and-justice Christians will realize.

Justice and Redistribution

The Religious Left's notion of justice fares no better. Traditionally, distinctions are made for three kinds of justice. First, interpersonal relations involving economic exchanges raise questions of *commercial justice*. When people exchange goods and services, questions arise as to whether the exchange is fair or the compensation just. Passages of Scripture like Leviticus 19:36 and Proverbs 16:11, which oblige merchants to have just scales and weights, seem directed to this type of justice. Second, instances when some wrong must be made right under either criminal or civil law are occasions for *remedial justice*. Exodus 23:3–6 is one of several biblical passages that speak to such issues. Finally, questions about *distributive justice* arise in situations where some good or burden is to be apportioned among human beings. Such situations are encountered frequently in life, as in the case of a parent who must decide how to divide the evening dessert among a large family. Or consider the case of a person who is preparing a will and deciding how to divide the estate among several heirs.

The Religious Left's writings about justice make it clear that they have been interested almost exclusively in questions of distributive justice. That is evident in their announced intention to help the poor. Trying to divide an estate equitably is an example of a voluntary kind of distributive justice. However, there is also an involuntary kind. Political liberals concerned with distributive justice on the level of an entire society usually try to disguise the fact that their goal must be enacted through governmental coercion.

On several occasions I have heard Ron Sider give eloquent appeals to rich Christians in America to use their wealth to help the poor. Sider deserves credit for encouraging people to share their possessions in a voluntary way. What he neglects to say is that he also expects the government to take people's money through taxation and redistribute it throughout society. Some of Sider's followers sensed that he was an apologist for higher taxes that would fund greatly expanded liberal social programs. Others seemed to miss this point and simply got caught up in the idealism of a noble crusade to help the poor.

There is obviously a big difference between Christians *voluntarily* giving their own money to fund nongovernmental programs to help the poor and the quite different situations in which agents of the state *take* the money, keep a large portion of it for salaries and bureaucratic administration,[25] and use some of what's left to fund counterproductive and self-defeating programs that end up making life even more miserable for the poor. In the words of one writer,

> The principal beneficiaries of the money absorbed and dispensed by government are not poor blacks in ghettos or Appalachian whites or elderly pensioners receiving Social Security checks—the usual figures conjured up when social welfare spending is discussed. The major beneficiaries, instead, are the *employees of government itself*—people engaged in administering some real or imagined service to the underprivileged or, as the case may be, the overprivileged. . . . The gross effect of increased government spending is to transfer money away from relatively low income people—average taxpayers who must pay the bills—to relatively high income people—Federal functionaries who are being paid out of the taxpayer's pocket.[26]

Members of the evangelical Left convinced themselves that the Bible commands a view of justice consistent with the values of political liberalism. Because Scripture frequently mentions justice in contexts that also refer to serving in love, helping the poor, and providing food for the hungry, it was easy for them to present a superficially plausible case for their position. But these appeals to Scripture should have been scrutinized more carefully. For example, some of the verses they quoted referred not to distributive justice, but to remedial justice. This is clearly true in the case of Exodus 23:6, which warns against depriving the poor man of justice but explains that the justice in view is the kind we expect to find in a court of law. The same chapter also warns against showing partiality *toward* the poor in a course of law (v. 3).

Another way the Religious Left have twisted the biblical call for justice was by reading twentieth-century meanings into the biblical text. The basic idea in the Old Testament notion of justice is righteousness, but the Christian leftists ignored this. When the Bible says that Noah was a just man, it does not mean that he would have voted the straight Democratic ticket; it means simply that he was a righteous man.

Old Testament prophets like Amos and Isaiah attacked prevailing forms of injustice, including dishonesty, fraud, theft, bribery, and exploitation of the weak, poor, and powerless. All these actions reflect a lack of personal righteousness. The prophets also denounced injustice on the level of social structure—for instance, an unjust legal system. In Scripture, both individuals and nations can be guilty of sin. But missing from these biblical calls for justice is any equivalent of the modern welfare state, in which government forcibly takes the possessions of some in order to give it to others. According to British economist Brian Griffiths, the Old Testament prophets

> never suggest that the remedy [for injustice] is therefore an economic redistribution conducted in some sort of spiritual vacuum. They invariably pinpoint the root cause of the trouble as spiritual: the nation has departed from God and economic injustice is one result. The priority therefore is not socio-economic but spiritual repentance. In this they showed great insight. Massive redistribution of wealth and complex laws to coerce the right to divest their properties would be of no avail whatever if there were not a simultaneous commitment on the part of those involved to change their values and behavior. It was this that the prophets saw as the basis for a just society.[27]

Christians are responsible for those they can help (Matt. 25:31–46). Jesus' disciples were to demonstrate a constant willingness to share their possessions with others (Luke 6:29–30). However, the New Testament says nothing about this sharing being coerced by the state.

Once Christians acknowledge their obligation to care about the poor and to take action on their behalf, the next question concerns the best means to do this. Christians may even agree that there are times when the poor will require help in the form of cash and noncash benefits in the short run. But they must be wary of any system of "aid" that encourages people to become dependent on the dole, that robs the poor of incentives to seek ways of helping themselves, and that leads the poor into a trap of perpetual poverty. Programs with such consequences are hardly models of genuine compassion or of wise public policy.

One of the more serious weaknesses in the Left's position is its confusion between justice and love. By its very nature, the state is an institution of coercion; it must operate through the use of force. Furthermore, when justice is involved, it must be dispensed impersonally. Not to act impersonally is to discriminate among persons, and such discrimination is an essential feature of injustice. This analysis of justice conflicts with the nature of love at a number of points.

For example, love must always be voluntary. No one can be forced to love. Moreover, love is always personal (not impersonal), in the sense that it is directed at specific individuals. Such discrimination on the part of the state would be a paradigm of injustice.

Love should also be willing to sacrifice, to go beyond the ordinary moral and legal requirements of a situation. A necessarily coercive state cannot serve as an instrument of love; the need to use force is incompatible with the nature and demands of love. As soon as the coercive state enters the picture, love must leave.

When Christian liberals confuse love with justice, they are doing more than simply urging others in society to manifest a compassionate love for the needy. They are in effect demanding that the state get out its weapons and force people to fulfill the demands of love. No Christian should favor compulsion in bringing people to theological commitment. But is voluntarism any less essential to social virtue? The political liberal's statist approach ignores *giving* and places all its emphasis on *receiving*, on who gets what. And of course, given the nature of statism, *giving* is supplanted by *taking,* a taking effected by the state through its powers of taxation.

While few Christians would disagree with the need to be concerned with issues of peace and justice, greater care should be given to how we unpack the meaning of these terms. And greater wisdom should be shown in the means we select to reach these ends. In the meantime, there is no reason to accept the claim that the Religious Left has a monopoly on the issues of peace and justice.

Chapter Nine

Tony Campolo and *Is Jesus a Republican or a Democrat?*

Tony Campolo wears many hats. He is a well-known author and sociology professor at Eastern College. He is also a dynamic Baptist preacher who is equally at home giving public lectures to civic organizations or sermons at evangelistic rallies. Campolo is very popular among young people, who flock to his messages. His skill at interweaving his liberal social convictions with his preaching enhances his influence among impressionable young people who often lack the ability to separate the biblical content in his messages from his personal, liberal political view of things.

I have already mentioned the strange coincidence surrounding the recent appearance of several books from leaders of the evangelical Left. These books not only appeared within the space of several months, but also strike a similar theme, each of them arguing among other things that their version of the Religious Left is really a new form of moderate centrism. We have noticed Jim Wallis's contribution to this agenda, *The Soul of Politics*. Tom Sine, another evangelical Left author, has published a book titled *Cease Fire*.[1] Tony Campolo's offering was his October 1995 publication, *Is Jesus a Republican or a Democrat?*[2]

This common theme was noticed in a recent review of Sine's book:

Ironically, in calling for a cease fire in the culture wars, the author ... enters the fray fully armed for rhetorical combat. To be sure, to protect his left flank he lobs a few random hand-grenades in the direction of what he calls the PC [politically correct] left.... But for the most part the book consists of well-aimed, highly concentrated fire on the Christian right and the Christian Coalition. He tries to hide his partisanship but just can't pull it off.... And then, if one has any doubts, he gives it all away by concluding the book with an extended advertisement for *Cry for Renewal*, a document written by Jim Wallis, editor of the evangelical left-wing journal *Sojourners*. When the writings of Wallis and other evangelicals long associated with the Christian left ... are offered up as a "radical biblical way that transcends the highly politicized agendas" of the Christian right and the PC left, one can't help but think that the whole thing is more than a little disingenuous.[3]

What is fascinating here is the ease with which many of the reviewer's comments about Sine's book apply to Campolo's new title. The latter must be examined by those who want to know what his version of evangelical Left thinking looks like at the moment.

IS JESUS A REPUBLICAN OR A DEMOCRAT?

If there is anything we have learned thus far, it is that sooner or later, representatives of the evangelical Left will proclaim that they are neither right nor left, neither conservative nor liberal. Campolo offers his own assertions along these lines in the preface to his book.[4] He attempts to blur the details of his liberal past by stating that he is now liberal on some matters and conservative on others. Although most people can say the same thing, the relevant point concerns the issues on which we are conservative or liberal. Campolo promises that he "will try to stand above both political parties as [he endeavors] to make judgments on issues according to the teachings of Scripture."[5] Of course, most Christian conservatives attempt to do the same thing.

The Seduction of Innocent Christians

Campolo warns that Democratic and Republican leaders want to seduce Christians into becoming part of their partisan programs. He alleges that the political parties "want to make the church a political block that can be delivered to the candidates of their choice. These politicians flatter us with their attention," he says, "and after having been ignored by them for so long, we are all too ready to fall for their flattery."[6] It is ironic that Campolo has seemed to abet this strategy by arranging meetings between President Clinton and prominent evangelicals, even though his statements in the book surely have Christian conservatives and their relationship with the Congress in mind.

The book's big announcement is that Jesus is neither a Republican or a Democrat—a truism probably prompted by conservatives who, in his opinion, do regard God as the former. But never once does Campolo offer a single quotation in support of this offensive claim.

Conservatism's Rise to Prominence

Campolo admits that liberals used to have a monopoly on political power in America, but concedes that the liberal monopoly has ended.

> Conservatism now appears to be the unstoppable social ideology. In both politics and religion ... the movement toward the right seems irresistible. The mainline churches with their social consciousness and their stellar liberal credentials find themselves in rapid decline. ... Suddenly, it seems as though God has switched political affiliations. These days, God seems to have become a deity owned by the Republican Party.[7]

Campolo's obituary for liberalism is premature. Liberals continue to dominate the scene in the hierachies of America's mainline Protestant denominations; they thrive in America's colleges, universities, and seminaries; and their fingerprints are all over the evangelical movement.

Praise and Blame for Both Parties

Since a self-described moderate like Campolo must appear neutral, he is obliged to offer praise and blame for both political parties. What is good about Republicans, Campolo suggests, is their emphasis on individual responsibility. This means, for example, that people should not blame others for problems resulting from their failings. As an example, he cites Republican criticisms of welfare cheats.

What does Campolo see as worthy in the Democratic party? "Democrats, on the other hand, are more likely to see the ways in which society can victimize people. Democrats are the ones who are likely to see how social structures can function unfairly to keep certain groups of people from being able to fully share in the American Dream."[8] Campolo's vision is again faulty. Millions of America's poor are forever cut off from participating in the American Dream because of their addiction to the paternalism of the welfare state.

"Democrats," Campolo continues, "are the ones most committed to ending those policies or practices that deny to any ethnic, economic, or gender group the equal opportunities that a just society should provide for all of its citizens. It is the Democrats who seem more than ready to try to correct past injustices suffered by those who have been the victims of prejudices."[9] Campolo's subject here, of course, is the liberal mantra of Affirmative Action, which translates into quotas and reverse discrimination against people who were never participants in earlier acts of discrimination. As hard as he tries, Campolo still has not rid himself of his liberal presuppositions and still can't see the way the world really is.

Weaknesses of Republicans

What are the weaknesses of the Republicans? Their rhetoric and attitude often seem mean, he says. What ought to concern Campolo, however, are the important ways in which Republican changes in failed liberal policies will benefit the poor. Campolo then adds that "Sometimes they [Republicans] fail to recognize that many individuals in this society cannot compete in our *laissez faire* economic system because they have been denied the chance to learn the skills and to develop the traits that make for social success. Some people who never really had a chance to succeed are labeled as losers."[10]

Campolo is silent about why so many people in this society cannot compete, although he acknowledges the complicity of liberal social programs in the breakup of many poor families. The absence of an adequate family structure in many poor homes is certainly one reason for the hopeless condition of many American youth. Most of the people who cannot compete are also handicapped by bad education. *Time* reported that 13 percent of American seventeen-year-olds (among minorities, 40 percent) are functionally illiterate—that is, unable to use language or numbers well enough to get along in society.[11] These people will naturally have trouble finding employment. Campolo is silent about the way the liberal educational establishment (including the liberals' favorite union, the National Education Association) has engaged in a systematic dumbing down of education in America.[12] Campolo's belief that liberals want to do something about people who cannot compete ignores liberal complicity in helping produce America's educational crisis. Campolo believes that the same government that helped to create these problems can now be trusted to solve them; conservatives disagree.

Democratic Weaknesses and Voluntary, Nongovernmental Action

As for the weaknesses of the Democrats, Campolo says they "often tend to see big government as the answer to every social problem. They seem reluctant to admit there is anything wrong with society in general or with individuals in particular that government cannot correct. It almost seems as though no one can dream up a new government program the Democrats do not like."[13] Finally, someone in the evangelical Left has caught the scent.

"Democrats," Campolo states, "often do not understand that, in the end, individual volunteerism encouraged by churches and civic groups (and not a host of new programs sponsored by Washington) is what is needed if we are going to solve the social problems that now overwhelm us."[14] Campolo continues:

> Most of the needs of those who are marginalized and left behind in the American race toward success cannot be met by government. Instead, our churches need to inspire their people to reach out to those around them who have fallen between the cracks and become part of the growing underclass of America. Unless Christians recognize their responsibility to the less fortunate, little progress can be made toward alleviating the sufferings of the socially disinherited. The privileged must carry out their "noble obligation" toward the underprivileged on a personal, caring level if we are even to begin to rescue those among us who seem to be drowning in hopelessness and despair.[15]

If the evangelical Left is serious about proposals like this, then real cooperation with conservatives may be possible.

Personal Salvation and Social Structures

According to Campolo, many Christians believe that all that is necessary to produce a good society is to get individual people saved. Many evangelical conservatives are trying to correct this kind of shallow thinking. Campolo is surely right when he adds, "We will never have a good society unless individuals are personally transformed by the Holy Spirit. But neither will we have a good society if we do not address the structural evils we find in the social arrangements of our time."[16]

Campolo is referring to the important difference between evil that results from the actions of individuals and that which results from unjust social structures. For example, the Nazis as individuals hated Jews (personal evil) and developed a system of laws that discriminated against them (unjust social structures). Little would have been accomplished if post-war Germany had rid itself of the Nazis but retained the unjust laws. Any nation can have a set of foolish or unjust institutional arrangements. Anyone who thinks that informed conservatives do not wish to address structural evils simply has not been paying attention.

One of Campolo's faulty assumptions, however, is that people only deal with structural evil when they do it in a liberal way. This false notion ignores the important difference between means and ends. Liberals and conservatives can agree on the correct ends (such as helping poor, uneducated, or unskilled people) but disagree about the best means to achieve those ends. Campolo fails to see how some structural evils result from bad liberal social policy.

Old Liberal Answers Won't Work

Campolo then discusses the ways in which Republicans attract him. "First, I agree with the Republicans that the old answers to social problems posed by political liberals during the sixties will not work."[17] The "old answers" of the sixties that Campolo finds inadequate happen also to be the "new answers" of the Democratic leadership in the mid-nineties. Following the lead of Jim Wallis and Ron Sider, Campolo contends we must find new ways to attack the nation's problems. Yet he admits that the discovery of these "new ways" is not something we can expect from the Democrats.

> Big government with its "top-down" programs is not going to be the primary means by which we can effectively respond to crime, premarital pregnancy, drug use, illiteracy, joblessness, divorce, alcoholism, child abuse, homelessness, and domestic violence. We need a new kind of politics that emphasizes localism.[18]

What Campolo means by "localism" is that we need to shift the focus away from the central government in Washington (the old way of the Democrats) and attack problems on a local or community level. Campolo recommends voluntary approaches that once again place churches and voluntary community organizations at the center of the process. "Local people working together can best understand and address the problems they encounter in their own neighborhoods."[19]

Campolo refuses to admit that the kind of vision he describes has been touted by conservatives for years. "The day when big, expensive programs to solve local problems are designed by government experts in Washington is over."[20] While conservatives join with Campolo in hoping this is so, they know only too well that a return to Democratic control of the Congress will resurrect the discredited approach of the past.

> I am calling for a new kind of politics that will give decision-making power back to neighborhood people.[21] These are the people who can make the best sense out of what is happening on their streets and who can best figure out what needs to be done to make things right. This does not mean that government dollars are not needed; it is just that government cannot be the primary social problem solver.[22]

Surprisingly, Campolo also gives Republicans credit for offering a sensible plan to "wipe out the national debt."[23] Since that *debt* now exceeds five *trillion* dollars, Campolo probably means that Republicans have the commitment and the ideas to eliminate the annual budget *deficit* that is the cause of the huge national debt. "We all see something morally wrong with spending programs that benefit us while building an unbearable debt that will crush our children and grandchildren."[24] Many grandparents who have reflected on the budget debacle have become fiscal conservatives. "Furthermore, Christians have biblical directives against debt and stand opposed to lifestyles that get people to live beyond their means. If a balanced budget is a Republican thing, then they are on to something that most Christians believe is part of the biblical ethic."[25]

WHAT SHOULD CHRISTIANS DO ABOUT THE WELFARE SYSTEM?

Campolo's discussion of the welfare system, the subject of chapter 16 in his book, brings forth some unexpected observations.

More than a half-century ago, the U.S. government initiated a welfare system. It was supposed to be a safety net for those who fell on bad times or had difficulties that prevented them from supporting themselves. During the years of President Lyndon B. Johnson, this basic welfare system was expanded into what came to be called the "Great Society" programs.

Sadly, what began as our honest and compassionate attempt to help the poor has turned into a nightmare of abuse and waste, Campolo admits. Campolo applauds the work of Charles Murray, a politically conservative economist, who outlined the impact of the Great Society programs in his book *Losing Ground*. With well-documented statistics, Murray makes his case that the welfare programs of the Great Society years only made things worse. Benefits offered by the welfare system were so generous that they discouraged people from getting jobs. For instance, according to one estimate, a person in the Los Angeles area would have to earn $7.50 an hour just to *equal* the benefits that welfare agencies would provide her or him in grants, food stamps, and services. Murray argues that for many people, the welfare system has destroyed all incentive to work.

Over the course of three decades, Campolo states, welfare has become a way of life for millions of Americans. There are huge numbers of able-bodied men and women who have shirked their responsibility to earn a living and learned to live off the labors of others.[26]

It is comforting to hear a member of the evangelical Left admit the failings of the welfare state, but it is also disturbing to remember that in times past, evangelical liberals treated support for this same welfare system as a litmus test of Christian spirituality and commitment to social justice.

"You don't have to be a right-wing Republican," Campolo now says, "to be horrified at what has happened to the welfare system. Even liberal Democrats are appalled by the situation."[27] Unfortunately, Campolo fails to identify any of these Democrats, nor have any statements about such a change of heart been reported in the media. To the contrary, demagogic speeches by Democrats against efforts to change the system continue.

Campolo contends "that hundreds of thousands of able-bodied men and women are on welfare because of ... the deindustrialization of America. Over the past quarter of a century ... either because of automation or the exporting of heavy industries to the Third World countries, America has lost huge numbers of high-paying jobs that were once available to semi-skilled laborers."[28] He is unable to see how much of this job loss is another consequence of liberal tinkering with the economy, another by-product of interventionist economics. In many cases, governmentally mandated costs (social security, family leave, minimum-wage laws, the Occupational Safety and Health Administration [OSHA], and the like) raised wage costs high enough to give many American businesses incentives to switch their manufacturing operations to other nations.

What can be done about the millions of unskilled workers who have only welfare or minimum-wage jobs to look forward to? Campolo believes that wise and caring churches can create jobs for such people. He offers a short list of businesses and micro-industries that could be started by churches or operated in church buildings. They include recharging cartridges for word processors and laser printers; rebuilding alternators and generators for automobiles; silk-screen printing of posters, T-shirts, and greeting cards; production of nails and other hardware items; production of fishing flies; moving businesses (trucks can be rented); and cleaning businesses.[29]

But once again, Campolo seems unaware of the economic realities. The church-run businesses will need money and equipment. Banks can be quite stubborn about loaning money to people who have no credit and little business experience. The businesses will also encounter significant costs imposed by government (such as social security taxes), oppressive red tape stemming from thousands of pages of governmental regulations, and frustrating obstacles from governmental agencies such as OSHA. If and when Christian churches ever attempt what Campolo recommends, they will quickly discover that their biggest enemy is the government. Campolo should hope that the Republican majority in Congress becomes large enough to eliminate many of these obstacles. I am not attacking the idea that voluntary groups like churches can and should help the poor by helping to provide jobs. My point is that Campolo seems to lack understanding of two things: (1) how liberalism's Big Government makes it difficult for business to succeed today, and (2) how complex and risky any business venture can be.

The "new ideas" Campolo recommends in his book are not new. When he recommends volunteerism and localism and urges churches and voluntary community organizations to get involved with poverty, unemployment, and other problems, he is simply signing on to ideas that conservatives (not liberals) have been promoting for years. In 1987 I wrote, "[T]he welfare system should be reformed so as to give proper recognition to the importance of such voluntary organizations and private charities."[30] Even then, this was hardly a new idea.[31] Conservatives have been promoting changes like this for decades.

According to the Center on Religion and Society, "The key institutions [in dealing with poverty] are the mediating structures of family, church, voluntary associations, and neighborhoods. Through these institutions, people are empowered to meet their own needs as they best understand their own needs. . . . Policies that strengthen the mediating structures are good; policies that weaken them are bad."[32] Liberals in Congress have excelled at finding ways to weaken such mediating institutions.

Perhaps conservatives shouldn't complain about Campolo's discovery of conservative social theory, but it hardly makes sense to allow people who have condemned conservative ideas for decades to suddenly adopt those ideas and present them as the evangelical Left's "new way of thinking."

International Issues in Economics

When it comes to economic problems on the international level, all Campolo can think of is giving Third World countries more U.S. dollars through what is misleadingly called foreign aid. He fails to see that there have been many unfortunate consequences of foreign aid. It often hinders economic development, frequently subsidizes destructive national policies, encourages consolidation of political power at the expense of individual free-dom, reinforces the myth that the reason some countries are rich is because they have exploited poor countries, and deceives people into thinking that benefits are available without the need to pay for them. Because so much can be gained by acquiring political power in a situation where millions of dollars of foreign money are channeled through governments, foreign aid can also lead to greater politicization in nations receiving it.[33]

CAMPOLO'S ATTACK ON CHRISTIAN CONSERVATIVES

It surprises no one that Campolo dislikes talk radio in general and Christian talk radio in particular. The reason: They are too conser-vative. While Campolo hints at a conspiracy, the real reason behind the conservative domination of talk radio must be that the listeners like it. Of course, liberals could change all this if a liberal Congress were to pass a law that allowed radio stations to be taken to court for violating some supposed principle of "equal access." Congres-sional liberals even talked about such a law in 1993. Privately, they referred to it as the "Get Rush [Limbaugh]" law. Such a law would have serious repercussions for freedom of speech in our nation.

Campolo complains that Christian talk radio is surreptitiously helping elect conservative candidates to political office, something that tax-exempt organizations are forbidden to do. No liberals complain, however, when minority churches and powerful labor unions do precisely this for liberal politicians. Campolo forgets that Ron Sider's *JustLife* magazines, published by a politically lib-eral tax-exempt organization, clearly pushed for the election of candidates supported by the Religious Left. Given the history of the Religious Left, Campolo's complaints about the content of Christian radio seem hypocritical.

Campolo saves his harshest criticism for the Christian Coali-tion, that allegedly dangerous, supposedly totalitarian group of Christian parents, grandmothers, Sunday school teachers, and preachers. Campolo thinks these people are shamelessly selling their souls to a political party that promises to curtail the power of those who seek to kill the unborn at will, among other things. He states, "We must not threaten our fellow citizens with a Christian takeover of society nor try to force them to capitulate to our rules."[34] It is hard to take Campolo's concerns seriously because they seem to be based on no more than rumors and innuendo. He has allowed his long-held liberal beliefs and attitudes to distort the meaning and significance of the deeds and statements of a few conservatives. He is maligning Christian brothers and sisters who are peacefully attempting to make the United States a better nation.

It is not Christian political involvement that frightens the evangelical Left; it is the fact that these Christians are conservatives—and successful.

Chapter Ten

Campolo's Responses to Four Questions

This chapter will examine Tony Campolo's way of dealing with four important issues—namely, homosexuality, feminism, the environment, and theological liberalism.

THE HOMOSEXUAL QUESTION

Campolo says that his preaching and lecturing ministries have suffered because of what he describes as his courageous stand on the homosexual question. It is natural to wonder what his position is on this controversial issue, but that is not easy to say. His published discussions suffer from at least three problems: (1) enormous vagueness at key points; (2) his difficulty in recognizing the logical implications of various things he says; and (3) the troubling sense that he repeatedly contradicts himself.

Three Positions Within the Church

Within official Christendom, three positions regarding a proper Christian attitude toward homosexual practice exist. The first and most liberal view repudiates any biblical passage that condemns same-gender sex and considers homosexuality an acceptable Christian "lifestyle." This is the view held by many liberals in mainline churches, but because of its stance on Scripture, it is not of great concern to our discussion in this book, which is interested primarily in evangelical opinions.

The second and third positions represent two radically opposed interpretations of what Scripture teaches about homosexual activity.[1] The historic Christian position has been that the Bible condemns same-gender sex along with other forms of sexual sin such as adultery and fornication (heterosexual conduct outside the bounds of marriage). Beginning in the sixties and seventies, some defenders of same-gender sex began to promote a form of biblical revisionism that set aside the church's traditional understanding of key Scripture passages dealing with homosexual activity. Stanton L. Jones, a psychology professor at Wheaton College, offers a glimpse at this new way of reading the homosexual passages in Scripture:

> They [homosexual revisionists] argue that Leviticus 18:22, 20:13, and Deuteronomy 23:18, which condemn male homosexual behavior, are irrelevant because they do not address today's homosexual lifestyles. These passages occur in the midst of a discussion of God's disapproval of the fertility cults in the pagan communities surrounding the Israelites. The only kind of homosexual behavior the Israelites knew, it is argued, was homosexual prostitution in pagan temples. That is what is being rejected here and not the loving monogamous gay relationship of persons of homosexual orientation today.
>
> The Genesis 19 story of Sodom and Gomorrah is alleged to be irrelevant because it is a story of attempted gang rape, which was an indicator of the general wickedness of the city. The homosexual nature of the gang rape is seen as an irrelevant detail of the story.
>
> Romans 1 is often reduced to being a condemnation solely of heterosexual people who engage in homosexual acts. They rebel against God by engaging in what is unnatural to them. This passage has no relevance today, it is argued,

because modern homosexuals are doing what is natural to them and thus not rebelling against God.

In 1 Corinthians 6:9 and 1 Timothy 1:10, the Greek words that are often translated as referring to homosexual practices are said to be unclear and probably describe and forbid only pederasty, the sexual possession of an adolescent boy by an older adult man of the elite social classes.[2]

Jones finds the revisionist's case unconvincing and remarkable, he says, because *"every time homosexual practice is mentioned in the Scriptures, it is condemned."*[3]

Within the evangelical Left, Ron Sider and apparently Campolo line up with the traditional Christian view that same-gender sex is sinful. *Sojourners* and such other evangelical Left publications as *The Other Side* and *The Daughters of Sarah* defend the revisionist position that homosexual activity between monogamous same-gender partners is not condemned by Scripture. The last group also argues for the ordination of practicing homosexuals.[4]

One probable reason that Campolo's ministry has suffered[5] is a perception that he accepts the revisionist position. Campolo has tried to clarify his views in a number of writings. His problem has been that even though each of these statements declares his belief that same-gender sex is wrong, he then appears to defend other views that seem incompatible with this claim.

In one of his books, for example, Campolo expresses his disagreement with the homosexual reading of Romans 1:26–27. He then admits that he still sees some legitimacy in the revisionist interpretation of what many regard as the clearest biblical passage on the question.[6] Campolo's handling of 1 Corinthians 6:9 and 1 Timothy 1:10 also finds him sympathetic to the pro-homosexual interpretation; he believes that in these verses Paul was only condemning adult men who seek sex with young boys (pederasty). "To compare pederasty," he writes, *"to a relationship chosen in love* is considered by [some Bible scholars] to be a serious mistake."[7]

If Campolo finds merit in the pro-homosexual reading of all the relevant Biblical passages, what is his reason for judging homosexual conduct as sin? Is this simply a sop thrown to the fundamentalists who read his books? It would appear that Campolo wants things both ways. On the one hand, he does not want evangelical readers to think he endorses or supports homosexual behavior. On the other hand, his tortured exegesis of Scripture leads to the conclusion that he really does not think Paul condemns such behavior.

A few pages later, Campolo adds to the confusion by proclaiming, "The fact that homosexuality has become such an overriding concern for many contemporary preachers may be more a reflection of the homophobia of the church than it is the result of the emphasis of Scripture."[8]

A big part of Campolo's problem is the careless way he introduces emotionally charged terms like "homophobia" into all of his discussions of homosexuality. In its literal sense, the word refers to a compulsive fear of homosexuals along with revulsion at the unnatural ways they engage in sex. Just as some people are terrified of heights, flying, black cats, and small rooms, this "phobia" refers to an abnormal, illogical, and pathological fear. However, homosexuals regard *any* criticism of their "lifestyle" as homophobic. I know people who have no more dislike of homosexuals than they do of people who pick their noses in public, yet, in Campolo's hyperactive vocabulary, such people are homophobes. This reckless use of language trivializes the term and hinders meaningful discussion.

Campolo published an article titled "What About Homophobia?" in the February 1994 issue of Ron Sider's publication, *Prism*. Campolo thinks that what he calls the "persecution" of homosexuals in society and in the church is "the dominant civil rights issue of the nineties."[9] He refers to increasing incidents of gay-bashing but fails to say whether all of the incidents involve verbal and physical violence or are simply polite refusals to associate. Actual or threatened violence and abusive language are un-Christian and deserve criticism. But when a person decides he would prefer to invite only Dallas Cowboy fans to his house to watch the Super

Bowl, that is hardly an act of discrimination. African-American economist Walter Williams tells how his decision to propose to the woman who became his wife entailed a kind of discrimination (in a greatly extended sense of the word) against every other woman in the world. Actions of this kind do not reflect any moral failing.

Campolo condemns Christians who distribute a video called *The Gay Agenda*. According to Campolo, "This video would have us believe that the obscene behavior of Queer Nation, a small group of troubled and offensive members of the homosexual community, is characteristic of the vast majority of our gay and lesbian friends."[10] Campolo then blames "homophobic" Christians for the obnoxious and obscene conduct of Queer Nation homosexuals. Such claims do not enhance Campolo's credibility, nor will they help him persuade typical evangelicals to alter their thinking about homosexuals.

Moreover, Campolo's extremely elastic account of homophobic behavior goes well beyond criticisms of rude and violent behavior. If a Christian college's stance on moral issues obliges it to expel any student found guilty of sinful heterosexual conduct (adultery or fornication), why should the college stop short of taking similar action with regard to same-gender sex, if—as Campolo repeatedly affirms in his writings—homosexual conduct is sin? If churches rightfully refuse people guilty of ongoing, unrepentant sinful heterosexual behavior access to church membership, leadership responsibilities, or ordination, how can Campolo complain when the same churches treat ongoing, unrepentant homosexual sin in the same way?

In the final paragraph of his *Prism* article, Campolo compares evangelicals who refuse to speak up for gay rights to the Christians in Germany who refused to condemn the Holocaust and the Nazi regime. He writes, "Those who remained silent about the Jews in Nazi Germany helped sign the death warrants of the Holocaust. Those who did not speak out for Blacks can be accused of allowing slavery to continue. . . . I believe that those who do not speak up for the gay and lesbian community at this crucial time in history may be lending support to oppression."[11]

Further complicating Campolo's views regarding homosexuality, he sees nothing wrong with people having a romantic attraction toward persons of the same sex. Nor does he think we should question the right of homosexual lovers to live together as long as they refuse to surrender to their homosexual desires. In truth, Campolo is far more critical of people he calls homophobic than he is of *any* homosexuals. He is especially angry toward people who fear that homosexual teachers might seduce students, as though this has never happened. Campolo surely is aware of those who are pushing to make homosexual behavior appear normal in America's schools.

As best as I can determine, Campolo appropriately wants Christians to condemn abusive language and violent behavior when dealing with homosexuals. But once we follow Campolo's lead and recognize the sinfulness of same-gender sex, the logical problems begin. Because a judgment of sinfulness implies moral condemnation, it is hard to see how consistent Christians can avoid speaking and acting in negative ways about homosexual conduct any less than sinful heterosexual behavior. It seems clear that Campolo is concerned that Christians not do or say anything that would harm or offend believers who, although having homosexual inclinations, admit that homosexual activity is sinful and therefore intentionally live in celibacy. Indeed, if properly tutored, many evangelicals can understand the importance of compassionately helping such people resist their temptations and grow in their faith, in the same way that Christians have learned to help those tempted by alcoholism, illegal drugs, gambling, or other addictions.

The most puzzling thing about Campolo's writings on the subject is his unusually narrow focus. Campolo is to be commended for standing up for repentant and born-again homosexuals who for conscience' sake live celibate lives. But, one is constrained to ask, what percentage of the homosexual population fits this description? A reasonable answer seems to be: less than one percent. Why does Campolo say so little about the other 99 percent? Why is he silent about homosexual activity too prurient to be described in this book? Why does he ignore the propensity of so many male homosexuals toward profligacy and anonymous sex? Why does he fail to discuss the refusal of so many homosexuals to take precautions against receiving and transmitting disease, including the HIV virus?[12] What is it about so many homosexuals knowingly infected with AIDS that leads them to lie about their condition to new sex partners? What is it about homosexuals knowingly infected with AIDS that leads them to become blood donors, aware that they are signing the death warrant of the innocent people who receive their blood?

Austin Pryor mentions the concern evangelicals have regarding the homosexual emphasis on having access to children.

> Consider these goals found in the Gay Rights Platform drafted by the National Coalition of Gay Organizations. Repeal all laws prohibiting sexual acts involving consenting persons (notice it does not say consent *adults*); repeal all laws governing the age of sexual consent; legislation that mandates child custody, adoption, and foster parenting shall not be denied because of sexual orientation; and, support for sex education courses, taught by gay men and women, presenting homosexuality as a valid, healthy preference and life-style.[13]

Why is Campolo silent about these concerns?

I have read somewhere that a homosexual with AIDS typically dies at about the age of forty, while a homosexual without AIDS dies about the age of forty-five. Is it cruel or homophobic to conclude that what is killing homosexuals is not AIDS but homosexuality? Is it homophobia or a sign of Christian love (*agape*) to want to see people rescued from this kind of life?

Stanton Jones wisely warns about the dangers of saying "the right things but in the wrong way."[14] Too many Christians, he states,

> have let hate slip into their rhetoric on this issue. The challenge here is to be the loving opposition, to imitate our Lord, who chases down his sinful creatures with aggressively open arms while all the while saying no to our sins. We all need to repent of our arrogant and intolerant attitudes toward those whose struggles are different from ours.

Our goal must be to become a community that embodies
the welcoming grace and love of our Lord Jesus Christ.[15]

One can only wish that Campolo's writings on the subject were as
clear and balanced as Stanton Jones' helpful article.

THE FEMINIST QUESTION

Many liberals have made a career of claiming that conservatives
do not believe in equality for women. It would be foolish to pretend that there is no disagreement among evangelical Christians
on this important issue. At the same time, it would be irresponsible to suggest that liberals hold a monopoly on concern about
equal treatment for women.

The issue is complicated by differing attitudes toward the
authority of Scripture, the proper interpretation of several key
passages in the Bible, and other matters. Not even the most rigid
traditionalist on male-female roles believes that men and women
differ in any essential way related to their humanity; at most, it is
a dispute over what Scripture may or may not teach about differing roles for men and women in the family, church, and society.

An oft-ignored but important distinction in the debate points
to the difference between two kinds of feminism. *Common-sense
feminists* believe that discrimination against any person (male or
female) on the basis of sex is wrong. Sensible feminists recognize
that there are some relevant differences between the sexes and
that some differences in roles are justifiable. There seem to be
good reasons, for example, to restrict the position of middle line-
backer on National Football League teams to men.

Gender-feminists, however, hold a much different attitude.
Radical or gender-feminism has as its ultimate goal the elimina-
tion of all distinctions between the sexes. As American philosopher
Christina Hoff Sommers explains, gender-feminism

is not primarily concerned with more opportunities for
women, or, for that matter, with including women's achieve-
ments in the [educational] curriculum. Its aim is to transform

our understanding of our past, our present and our future. How? By convincing people to accept the central insight of contemporary feminist philosophy: that the sex/gender system is the most important aspect of human relations.[16]

Gender-feminists, Sommers explains,

share an ideal of a genderless culture that inspires their rejection of such entrenched social arrangements as the family, marriage and maternal responsibilities for child rearing. They also call not only for a radical re-ordering of society but . . . a revolution in knowledge itself, which would extirpate [alleged] masculine bias, replacing the "male-centered [college curriculum]" with a new curriculum inspired by a radical feminist perspective.[17]

Tony Campolo has recently stated that his defense of feminism sides with the common-sense position and that he rejects gender-feminism.[18] *Sojourners* magazine appears to see nothing wrong with the radical feminist position on the family and the move of many toward pantheistic and otherwise pagan views of God. But, I repeat, once the extremism of radical feminism is removed from the table, the dispute over male-female roles is not an essential feature of the disagreement between the evangelical Right and Left. It is not an issue that by itself will turn an evangelical conservative into a liberal or vice versa.[19]

THE ENVIRONMENTAL QUESTION

Because both Tony Campolo and Ronald Sider have written extensively about the environment, my discussion of the topic could have been linked to either name.[20] I deal with it here largely because Campolo's treatment appeared in a book.

Both Sider and Campolo claim to recognize the dangers of enviromental extremism, especially the tendency of some to link it to pantheism, the worship of nature in place of God, and an antibiblical elevation of all forms of life to an equal status with human beings. Sider seems to understand these dangers more clearly than Campolo, however, whose book on the subject occasionally lapses into confusion.

Wilbur Bullock, a retired professor of zoology at the University of New Hampshire, has expressed reservations about Campolo's book. He notes that Campolo often bases his claims "on some very selective manipulation of Scripture as well as reliance on considerable nonbiblical emotional mysticism."[21] Bullock puzzles over Campolo's tendency to worry that worms might feel pain and that hateful talk might lead plants to wither and die.

Bullock is especially troubled by Campolo's casual indifference to his own warnings that Christians should not regard all life as equally valuable. According to Campolo, "One of the ways Christians can demonstrate their readiness to be led by the Holy Spirit is by making a commitment to the animal rights movement."[22] Campolo seems to endorse the Eastern Orthodox idea that "One of the consequences of Satan's work is that the evolutionary process has gone haywire. That is why we have mosquitoes, germs, viruses, etc. God did not create these evils. They evolved because Satan perverted the developmental forces at work in nature."[23] To Bullock, this theory implies that many "mean" features of nature were not created by God,[24] a suggestion he finds inconsistent with Psalm 104:21.

The summary verdict of this evangelical scientist on Campolo's book is less than complimentary:

We *need* to be concerned with rescuing the earth. We *will* be held responsible as stewards for what we have done to counter the effects of sin on God's creation. We must attempt this "rescue" on biblical terms. "Nature" is God's creation—nature is *not* God. Mankind is to *use* but not *abuse* nature. In spite of his excellent title, Campolo's approach is too close to worshipping nature. For that reason I cannot recommend this book as a real contribution to the *Christian* approach to environmental problems.[25]

Evangelical conservatives care about the environment. No one I know wants people to drink dirty water, breathe polluted air, eat carcinogens for dinner, or ignore actions that might cause global warning.[26] Liberals do not have a monopoly on concern for the environment. Informed conservatives do, however, tend to think more deeply than liberals. They have repeatedly drawn attention, for example, to the hidden religious and political agendas of many enviromentalists, a fact suggested by the title of a recent book, *Saviors of the Earth?*[27] Conservatives are also concerned about allegations of bad or unsupported "scientific" claims used to advocate extremist environmentalist programs.

Three major branches of radical environmentalism exist, commonly known as the Greens, the Deep Ecologists, and the Animal Rights Movement. The group known as the *Greens* are the most politically sophisticated, a fact that explains the care they take to hide their true agenda from the public. This movement has become the new home for hard-line socialists who want coercive governments to function as the new front for destroying private property rights. It hardly seems an accident that Mikhail Gorbachev, who never renounced his Communist beliefs, now works for "The Green Cross." Political and social radicals applaud the implicit revolutionary nature of contemporary environmentalism; they see it as a way of mobilizing the masses into promoting their radical agenda.

The *Deep Ecologists* are pantheistic fanatics with New Age, Hindu, or Buddhist overtones. They are represented by such organizations as "Greenpeace" and "Earth First."

The *Animal Rights Movement,* a group that Campolo urges Christians to support, is also pantheistic. It believes all of life is one, indivisible whole. No form of life is better than another. One of its favorite terms is "speciesism," which it defines as a bias for one's own species against others. In its view, humans are the only creatures who can be guilty of speciesism, which makes it the radical enviromentalist's corollary to racism and sexism. The best-known organization representing this movement is People for the Ethical Treatment of Animals (PETA).

Radical environmentalists are motivated by various forms of "profit." In some cases, the motivating factor is money. In 1992 the top twelve environmental groups raised $638 million. Six-figure salaries abound in the offices of these organizations. A second motivating factor is the political agenda of a new breed of socialists who regard private ownership of property as a major source of evil on the planet. A third motivating factor is the New Age religion of people in the Greenpeace and Earth First organizations. Not surprisingly, the National Council and World Council of Churches have ties to various environmentalist groups.

Christians need to show more discernment when joining various environmentalist movements. Radical organizations have always found ways of using impressionable, unthinking people to follow their lead. The importance of recognizing the hidden, often anti-Christian agendas of some of these groups cannot be emphasized too much.[28]

Concerned Christians also need to be aware of the abundance of bad science that is behind many environmentalist claims. Regrettably, Vice President Albert Gore's book *Earth in the Balance*[29] provides many textbook examples of dependence on questionable science, and this in turn has led too many evangelicals to pursue policies of environmental extremism instead of digging more deeply for the truth.

There is no room here to explain examples of bad science, but one book that does so very skillfully is *Eco-Sanity*, co-authored by Joseph L. Bast, Peter J. Hill, and Richard C. Rue.[30] While none of the co-authors question Vice President Gore's sincerity, they do suggest that he uses numbers erroneously, relies on questionable sources, and advocates extreme measures seldom justified by the facts. *Eco-Sanity* refers to Gore's position as the "'kitchen sink' theory of environmental policy design: do everything, all at once, regardless of cost or necessity."[31] Many of *Eco-Sanity*'s criticisms apply with equal force to Campolo's book, which often echoes Mr. Gore's theories.

The biggest barrier to securing better environmental protection, according to *Eco-Sanity*, "*is the environmental movement itself.*"[32] The authors explain:

[W]e believe the lack of understanding and critical thinking on the part of most environmentalists has compromised the movement's ability to be an effective force for environmental protection. Many environmentalists don't think clearly about the issues, relying instead on environmental organizations to do their thinking for them. This trust has been rewarded with campaigns against "crises" that don't exist and support for policies that are clumsy, expensive, and sometimes counterproductive. Similarly, environmentalists have said *let the government do it* ... and then they failed to pay attention to what the government actually did. A closer look quickly reveals that government's record on the environment is a poor one, and that government often suffers from perverse incentive structures and information blackouts that render it an unreliable ally of the movement.[33]

The authors conclude their book by stating: "The environment is cleaner than at any time in the past half century. The environment is safer than at any time in recorded history. Life expectancy has never been longer. Cancer rates are falling, not rising. Predictions of impending global ecological disasters are unproven. Most environmental problems have been or are being solved. Ideas are more important than things. Prosperity is good for the environment."[34]

Such claims, of course, run contrary to current environmentalist sentiment. Ideologues of the environmentalist movement will dispute such claims without bothering to examine the arguments and the evidence. Prudent Christians who care about the environment will avail themselves of the opportunity to examine the other side of this complex issue.

THE THEOLOGICAL QUESTION

One disturbing feature of the evangelical Left is its almost total silence about theological liberalism. Earlier in the book, I asked if political liberals like Wallis, Sider, and Campolo are afraid of alienating their natural political allies who are theologically liberal.

This inattention or indifference to what some would call theological apostasy becomes evident in another recent book by Campolo, *Can Mainline Denominations Make a Comeback?*[35]

The mainline churches have been losing members at such a rapid rate that one pundit has suggested that his own denomination will simply cease to exist about the year 2030.[36] Another has taken to taping computer-generated signs on the walls of such churches, reading, "Will the last member of this denomination to leave please turn out all the lights?" Many believe the mainline denominations have no future until they return to the essential doctrines of the historic Christian faith.

While Campolo's book deals with the decline of the mainline churches, he says nothing about the role that theological liberalism has played in their rapid loss of members. Even when Campolo suggests that the mainline churches could learn from evangelicalism, he does not have doctrine in mind. He only thinks they might be wise to consider adopting evangelicalism's emphasis on personal conversion and pastoral care. Unfortunately, he leaves the meaning of "personal conversion" ambiguous.

The fatal flaw of Campolo's book is what Robert Patterson calls his "blind spot regarding the theological nature of the mainline problem."[37] Patterson, himself a member of the mainline Presbyterian Church, U.S.A., chides Campolo by writing:

> Like a fossil from the 1960s, he clings to the liberal dream. . . . Consequently, he at times advances what *First Things* calls the Mainline Tale, interpreting declining numbers as a cost of "faithfulness." Seemingly oblivious to the disasters of ecclesiastical gifts to the Communist Party in the 1960s or feminist excesses in the 1990s, Campolo proudly proclaims that "history will attest to the fact that mainline churches did not 'play chicken' at a crucial time in American history."[38]

If the mainline churches believe Campolo's words are the only advice they need at this time of crisis, then their remaining time on the stage of Christendom may truly be short.

CONCLUSION

Now that our examination of the views of Jim Wallis, Ron Sider, and Tony Campolo is finished, we can draw some preliminary conclusions. Sider and Campolo do appear to be moderating their views on important issues, even though they are both reluctant to admit publicly that these changes affect radical and liberal beliefs that they once used as criteria of Christian faithfulness. They are noticeably silent about their political support for liberal politicians and policies in the past. They have not even come close to naming conservative pro-life candidates that they would now support. Their new emphasis on encouraging churches and other local volunteer organizations to deal with issues of poverty, hunger, unemployment, and addiction is a welcome move that increases the possibility of serious dialogue with conservatives. Their failure to admit (or at least recognize) the conservative roots of this kind of thinking is a bit disconcerting. What they tout as new approaches are not new at all.

Jim Wallis is another matter, however. While he has adopted the centrist rhetoric, many people think he has some serious repenting to do before he can assume a position of responsible leadership in any truly centrist movement. Many former radicals who shared Wallis's far left ideology have grown up, admitted their errors, and changed their ways. We still await evidence that Wallis is anything other than a quasi-Marxist attempting to jump-start his career. It is disconcerting to realize that Jim Wallis, the major American supporter of the *Road to Damascus* document, was the author of *The Cry for Renewal*.

Several troubling issues remain. One is the matter of evangelical liberals' long association with very questionable people on the left. A distinguishing feature of the Religious Left has been their tendency to work closely with people and organizations that have suspicious ties to pro-Communist, anti-American movements.[39] Even after we acknowledge the decent motives of the evangelical Left over all these years, the fact remains that these good individuals have played around with lots of bad people.

Chapter Eleven

The Silence of the Lambs: President Clinton and the Evangelical Left

One thing we have learned thus far is that American evangelicals are badly divided over how their personal faith should relate to matters in the public arena. It should not surprise us, therefore, that they are also divided over questions related to the character and competence of President Clinton. The evangelical Left, so far at least, has tended to support him and his administration; Christian conservatives have not.

Unlike many members of the secular and religious Left, I have enormous respect for the high office of President of the United States.[1] But respect for the office does not mandate silence about misconduct on the part of the person holding the position. That is beyond dispute.

Many people believe that even if President Clinton engaged in activities, while he was governor of Arkansas, that are morally or legally questionable, they are now ancient history and he should be judged solely on the basis of what he has done since becoming president. There are at least three reasons why this is simplistic. First, the allegations speak directly to the issue of the President's character. One does not have to be religious to believe that character matters. Second, if the allegations about certain past activities are true, then the White House has lied repeatedly about these matters. This moves the moral question from the past into the present. Finally, members of Congress have begun to mention the possibility of a White House coverup that amounts to obstruction of justice (a felony), a charge that if true refers to present events. Even if we ignore allegations of President Clinton's alleged adulteries during his Arkansas years, the remaining problems look very much like the sorts of things that produced the resignations of Richard Nixon and Spiro Agnew.

Some might argue that while all this material is newsworthy and worthy of discussion somewhere, it has no place in a book like this. I disagree. To ignore the evangelical Left's relationship to the President would be an irresponsible surrender to political expediency.

For two decades, members of the evangelical Left have portrayed themselves as modern descendants of the Old Testament prophets. Their repeated attacks on American institutions and individuals have been couched in moral tones. The real prophets of the Bible never allowed wealth, power, or high office to compromise the prophetic message. Is it irrelevant to raise questions about self-described twentieth-century prophets who consort with people who are said to have done immoral and illegal things, who have promoted public policies that contribute to the moral decline of the nation, and who may yet be indicted on felony charges? If I regarded myself as a modern-day descendant of Elijah and Amos, I believe I would be more careful about my relationship with people in high places, especially in light of the possibility of dishonoring my faith and the causes I hold dear.

The White House has been making a concerted effort to court evangelicals, at least those sympathetic to political liberalism. One cannot discount the possibility that one hidden agenda of the evangelical Left's recent push for national attention has the reelection of President Clinton as one of its objectives. No book on this subject can be deemed responsible if it fails to discuss candidly the questions that continue to be raised about the President and First Lady.

The question then turns to the appropriate ways in which fair and truthful people should report such matters, especially when the most serious allegations are the subject of ongoing congressional and prosecutorial investigation. A responsible author will make a clear distinction between facts and allegations. Congressional subpoenas are facts. Public statements by journalists and politicians are also facts, even though the content of those statements may still be allegations.

THE DIVIDED HOUSE OF MODERN EVANGELICALISM

Philip Yancey, a columnist for *Christianity Today*, admits to being "sobered by the alienation that exists between evangelicals and the current [Clinton] administration."[2] What sobers many evangelicals is Yancey's expression of surprise and displeasure at such news. Secular and religious liberals apparently find it hard to understand why so many evangelicals fail to be enamored by Clinton's persona and policies. After all, does he not care about the poor, the elderly, the infirmed, the hopeless, and the children? Has he not stated that he feels their pain?

Conservative evangelicals tend to doubt Clinton's sincerity. They also know how effective compassionate-sounding statements are to the large number of American voters who are basically uninformed about the many technical issues related to poverty, the budget, the economy, and international events. They also have enormous doubts about Clinton's character. His repeated flip-flops on issues, often within the same week, appear to them to be signs of incompetence and disrespect for the truth.

The high hopes the religious Left had for Clinton's administration is understandable. It may be difficult for future historians to recreate the ecstasy the American Left felt when what they called "the twelve years of Reagan-Bush" ended with the inauguration of William Jefferson Clinton in January 1993. What made the taste of Clinton's victory even sweeter was their belief that finally one of their own was in the White House. Clinton's evasion of the draft was for them a sign of honor. Cowardice had nothing to do with it—he hated the war as they had. Liberals who helped elect Jimmy Carter in 1976 and worked so hard for George McGovern, Walter Mondale, and Michael Dukakis now had a person like themselves in control of the executive branch of government; not only that, but Democratic liberals controlled the Congress.

THE ALLEGATIONS

During the presidential campaign of 1992, the Clinton team had to deal with three different types of allegations. The first concerned charges of numerous adulterous affairs.[3] During 1995, information leaks told of campaign staffers whose major responsibility was heading off problems from what Clinton's own aides called "Bimbo eruptions." Gennifer Flowers's efforts received some media attention with her tapes of intimate conversations with then-Governor Clinton. The campaign reportedly hired a private investigator to deal with other women. They failed in the case of Paula Jones, whose effort to sue the President for sexual harrassment resulted in the case's being delayed.[4]

Clearly, however, few Americans and even fewer members of the evangelical Left seem to care about that alleged sexual misconduct, at least until Miss Jones finally has her day in court.[5] Many evangelicals and Catholics believe this indifference disregards the serious questions these charges raise about the character of the man.

The second set of allegations concerned Clinton's evasion of the draft and his antiwar activities while a student in England.[6] The release of a photocopy of a letter Clinton wrote to his draft board—a letter that he thought had been destroyed—has led many to view his steps to avoid military service as devious. Yet, the antiwar activity and the draft evasion are ignored by many people even though others believe they raise additional questions about President Clinton's character.

The third set of allegations during the campaign concerned complex financial and real estate matters related to Clinton's investment in the Whitewater land deal. This is a problem that will not go away and could yet derail Clinton's reelection.[7]

THE WHITEWATER AFFAIR

During the first two years of the Clinton presidency, media liberals who supported him dismissed the Whitewater affair as much ado about nothing. The business transactions were too complex for them to understand and, besides, they contended, the voters proved they didn't care when they elected Clinton president. As long as the Democrats controlled Congress in 1993–94, Republican efforts to have the complex affair investigated met with stubborn resistance. When the elections of 1994 swept Republicans into control of the Congress, new information began to leak out.

The discovery that Mrs. Clinton had fortuitously turned a $1000 investment in the volatile cattle futures market into $100,000 interested neither the media, liberal Washington insiders, nor the evangelical Left. The silence of the evangelical Left was unusual, given the haste with which they traditionally respond to signs of greed and corruption. Media liberals refused to follow up on the strange connections between Mrs. Clinton's broker and major sources of money and power in the state of Arkansas. Whatever the truth about her financial bonanza, some wonder about possible conflicts of interest. Conservative publications have commented upon the possibility of "Cattlegate" being a cleverly disguised form of bribe. If this were ever proven, it would place "Cattlegate" in the same class of events that led to the downfall of Richard Nixon's vice president, Spiro Agnew.

The strange death of a presidential aide, Vincent Foster, has raised other questions. The mysterious disappearance of papers from Foster's White House office after his death is the subject of two congressional investigations. If there is nothing here, critics ask, Why the extraordinary White House effort to cover it up? Other charges concern the appearance of a possible conspiracy to obstruct justice within the presidential inner circle, based on the illegal use of confidential information about ongoing investigations and secret grand jury testimony.

At the end of 1995, even reluctant liberals in the media were beginning to pay more attention to Whitewater and associated matters—what John H. Fund referred to in the *National Review* as the end of a two-year period of media hibernation on these affairs.[8] What finally roused many reporters was the White House's claim of "executive privilege" in refusing to turn over notes on a Whitewater meeting in response to a Senate subpoena. Both the *Washington Post* and *New York Times* have even used the word "Watergate" in stories about recent White House actions.[9] Columnist Chris Matthews of the *San Franciso Examiner,* who had been an aide to former House Speaker "Tip" O'Neill, is quoted as saying: "It's a coverup of something. It has all the trappings of Watergate without the break-in. We don't know what went wrong, but we know something doesn't smell right."[10] Later on, Matthews again mused publicly about the Clintons' odd behavior:

> Something stirred Hillary Rodham Clinton's desire to keep the papers of White House deputy counsel Vincent Foster from police investigators in the hours after his suicide. Make your own list: lingering worries about a dicey tax matter; records of her highly lucrative commodity trading; the Clinton role in the White House travel-office episode; the Clinton investment in the Whitewater land development project; Mrs. Clinton's records as attorney for the Madison Savings and Loan; or some personal matter. Whatever combo of the above, the First Lady and White House lawyers paid a heavy price by keeping it from the police. If it was worth that much to them, it will have far more street value to Sen. Al D'Amato of New York.[11]

In early 1996, one hears the familiar Watergate phrase "obstruction of justice" more frequently in connection with Whitewater. According to John Fund,

> There are three standards by which one can judge the Clintons on Whitewater: legal, which means whether or not they committed actual crimes; ethical, which involves whether they have acted in a way appropriate to their high station in life; and political, which concerns whether the

American people feel Mr. Clinton should be trusted with another four years in office. . . . On the issue of ethics, the parallels between this Administration and that of Richard Nixon are almost eerie and are likely to inspire at least a couple of television documentaries.[12]

Fund concludes his article with this observation:

This time around, the media may not give the First Family a free pass. What is certainly true is that reporters who it some- times seemed would become interested in Whitewater only if there was evidence that the President and First Lady had robbed a bank in broad daylight are now focusing on why the White House consistently acts as if it has something to hide.[13]

It is impossible, at the time of this writing, to predict how any of this will play out, especially because of the strange disappear- ance of so many relevant documents. Whatever the truth turns out to be in these matters, it should be obvious that Christian con- servatives who get their information from outside the dominant liberal media believe some or many of the allegations about the peculiar behavior of the President and First Lady. So, too, it seems, do many liberal Washington insiders, as the inside-the- Beltway talk shows indicate.[14]

Has my handling of all this been fair? I believe so. When long- time liberals like Chris Matthews begin to suspect that something strange is going on, it would be inexcusable for evangelicals of either the Left or the Right to pretend otherwise.

THE STRANGE CASE OF JOYCELYN ELDERS

One supposes that President Clinton wishes he had never acceded to Mrs. Clinton's recommendation of Joycelyn Elders to become U.S. Surgeon General. Long after the President demanded her resigna- tion,[15] many people will continue to regard Dr. Elders as a symbol of a persistent problem in the Clinton psyche—namely, a weakness of judgment. Her policies and public pronouncements had proved con- troversial long before she became the Surgeon General.

As governor, Clinton had appointed Dr. Elders public health director for the state of Arkansas, a position she held from 1987 to 1993. In that capacity, she pursued policies promoting condoms in schools and abortion on demand. While incidents of teenage pregnancy, sexually transmitted diseases, and abortions in Arkansas had decreased under her predecessors, they increased dramatically during her tenure.

In January 1994, as the Surgeon General, Dr. Elders told the *New York Times Magazine* that "We really need to get over this love affair with the fetus and start worrying about children." In March 1994, she told *The Advocate*, a magazine for homosexuals, that homosexual sex is "a normal and healthy part of our being." She condemned the Boy Scouts of America for their refusal to permit homosexuals to act as scoutmasters. Elders referred to opponents of abortion as "non-Christians with slave-master mentalities."[16] She described pro-life advocates as people who "love little babies so long as they are in someone else's uterus." In June 1994, while serving as keynote speaker for the Lesbian and Gay Health Conference, Dr. Elders blamed the AIDS epidemic on the "un-Christian religious Right," not on the sexual practices of the people in her audience. And in 1994 she told *USA Weekend* that President Clinton told her, "I keep up with you everywhere you go and what you've been doing. I love it."

Elders's nomination as Surgeon General was opposed by such groups as Concerned Women for America, the American Family Association, the Christian Coalition, the Traditional Values Coalition, the Southern Baptist Convention Christian Life Commission, the Eagle Forum, the National Right to Life Committee, and the Catholic League for Religious and Civil Rights. The Catholic League charged Elders with attitudes toward the Catholic Church that are "inimical at best, and downright hostile at worst."[17]

RALPH REED ON BILL CLINTON

Probably no one reflects conservative evangelical attitudes about Bill Clinton more accurately than Ralph Reed, the holder of a Ph.D. in history who became president of the Christian Coalition.

My account of Reed's views is taken from a chapter in his 1994 book, *Politically Incorrect*.

Reed refers repeatedly to Clinton's problems with the twin issues of trust and character, by which Reed means our trust and Clinton's character. Reed suggests that part of the reason for the crises that have afflicted Clinton's administration results from the generational gap between him and older Americans whose values reflect an America rapidly disappearing from view. "What happens," Reed asks, "when yesterday's rebel becomes today's leader?"[18]

"In the final analysis," Reed observes,

> the authority of the president flows not from the ceremonial trappings of the office but from the character of the individual. This is where Clinton leaves many voters feeling cheated. And it explains why both the Whitewater scandal and allegations of sexual misconduct have resonated so powerfully in the electorate. They confirm an impression voters have of Clinton as less than forthcoming. . . . No single revelation—Whitewater, the Paula Jones [sexual harassment] law suit, commodities profiteering [also known as Cattlegate]—is fatal by itself. Instead, it is death by a thousand cuts, a series of episodes that confirms the reservations of voters about Clinton's character.[19]

Equally serious is the lack of trust Americans have in Clinton. Clinton "made a middle-class tax cut one of the central and most conspicuous promises of his campaign; yet in 1993, he passed one of the largest tax increases in history. He forswore U.S. involvement in Bosnia, then initiated air strikes that threatened to suck American forces into the conflict."[20] And now he has sent thousands of U.S. ground troops into Bosnia, a lethal trap reminiscent of the Vietnam situation that led him to evade the draft and protest that war. Critics suggest that Clinton hopes a show of militarism on his part will convince many 1996 voters that he has backbone, after all.

"During his State of the Union address in 1994," Reed continues, Clinton "spoke passionately about the need to restore traditional values and strengthen the family. Yet he favors paying for abortion with tax dollars and publicly advocates gay rights legislation. . . . The result is a president who inspires respect for his political skills but nothing else."[21]

Reed notes some similarity between Clinton's skill as an orator and Ronald Reagan. "The difference, of course, is that Reagan actually believed in something. He had a set of core beliefs that animated him, defined him, and provided a compass in the howling crosswinds that is the presidency. Clinton has no such center. His north star is charm itself—ingratiating, primordial, almost suffocating. He is like the boy that a girl brings home from a date who proceeds to flirt with her sister."[22] In Reed's analysis, "Clinton combines the earnestness of a Baptist Sunday school teacher with the smooth arrogance of an Oxford graduate student. Indeed, like a secular Elmer Gantry, he presents the ultimate triumph of rhetoric over reality, style over substance, charisma over character."[23]

Reed refers to Clinton's facility for rapid and repeated reversals of position even while he continues to persuade millions of people of his sincerity. Reed disagrees with those who believe "Clinton's inability to tell the truth is pathological."[24] This is too simplistic for Reed. In Reed's view, Clinton knows the truth: "He simply does not believe that it serves his purposes to tell it."[25]

Bill Clinton's work in the George McGovern presidential campaign of 1972, according to Reed, is one of two defining moments in his development. Like Jim Wallis and other members of the evangelical Left who were around then, Clinton brought an enthusiasm to his work that was the equal of any of the young radicals of the time. Hillary Clinton was also part of that crusade.

During his first term as the governor of Arkansas, Reed continues, Clinton temporarily dropped his moderate persona and not only revealed his true liberal convictions but did so in a decidedly arrogant way. The voters of Arkansas, disillusioned by the liberal they had chosen to govern them, threw Clinton out of office when he ran for reelection in 1980. While some said Clinton's political career was finished, Reed reports that Clinton worked diligently to refashion himself as a moderate.

Reed details the way Clinton repositioned himself:

Hillary Rodham adopted her husband's last name ... [as a] bow to the state's traditional views of marriage. . . . Bill began attending the largest Baptist church in Little Rock, even joining the choir where his beaming face could be seen on Sunday morning telecasts that reached half the state's population. It was during this period that Clinton began adopting the rhetoric of a "new" Democrat, emphasizing law-and-order, education reform, moving people off welfare, and even switching his position to support the death penalty. He made television spots in which he repented for the arrogance of the past. This conservative makeover worked like a charm: Clinton won the governor's race in 1982 with 54.7 percent of the vote.[26]

In Reed's view, "Bill Clinton suffers from a classic case of political schizophrenia. His core beliefs are those of a William Fullbright liberal radicalized by the twin experiences of Vietnam and the McGovern campaign. But his defeat in 1980 forced him to reposition himself. Clinton personifies the crisis of a political chameleon. This in great measure, explains his indecisiveness, his obvious frustration in exercising leadership, and the chaos that reigns in the White House under Clinton."[27]

Reed believes Clinton's greatest legacy was the way he gave conservatives cause to become active again. "The conservative community, largely asphyxiated during the Bush years, awoke from its slumber like Rip Van Winkle on steroids after the Clinton inaugural. Membership for pro-family organizations is up dramatically, attendance at conferences and seminars is rising, and the circulation of conservative publications is skyrocketing. . . . The Christian Coalition entered the Clinton era with 250,000 members and activists; that number now approaches 1.4 million."[28] Many liberals begrudgingly admit that Reed's analysis makes sense.

CLINTON AND "THE GANG OF TWELVE"

In spite of everything we have noted, many evangelical leaders approve of Clinton and his administration. In October 1993, about a dozen of them, singled out for invitations by Clinton's "good friend," Tony Campolo, had a breakfast meeting in the White House with the President and Vice President. The subsequent controversy over what other evangelicals regarded as their unseemly obeisance to the seductions of political power led to their being dubbed "the evangelical gang of twelve." The label is misleading in certain respects. The dozen evangelicals referred to were only part of a larger group of religious leaders who shuffle in and out of the White House at regular intervals. The term also implies that every person who was part of that October contingent was taken in by the effort, but some clearly were not.

In the *National Review*, Rich Lowry pondered the question of why Clinton began to pander to evangelicals. He found the answer, not in any inward religious commitment on Clinton's part, but rather in the numbers. Evangelicals, he explained, "account for a full quarter of the American electorate, and especially in the South and in the border states, are the rock upon which Republican presidential victories are built."[29]

It was President Bush's loss of evangelical support in the 1992 election that contributed to his electoral defeat in such states as Georgia, Louisiana, Kentucky, Missouri, Ohio, and Illinois. Independent candidate Ross Perot obtained almost 16 percent of the evangelical vote, while Clinton won even less (28 percent) than Democrat Michael Dukakis did in 1988.

The numbers mean that no one should have been surprised when Clinton invited "the gang of twelve" to the White House. Most of them were apparently impressed by the surroundings, the trappings of power, Clinton's personal way with them, and Clinton's seeming interest in how they could minister to his religious life. As Lowry notes, "That October breakfast produced gobs of the material James Carville must dream about."[30]

California pastor and television preacher Jack Hayford related to his congregation how he was asked to begin the breakfast round-table—having told a White House volunteer the night before how God had filled him with love for Clinton right after the 1992 election. Hayford described Clinton as less political than he expected, and he concluded by saying that Clinton is "a great man, a gifted man.... I know that I was talking to a brother in Christ and I'm glad the Lord allowed me a chance to serve in a small way."[31] The risks of a Christian minister talking this way about someone who may still face serious ethical or legal charges ought to be obvious.

Tony Campolo advised the group that Clinton "wants to cooperate with evangelicals in the task of rebuilding America."[32] Robert Seiple, the president of World Vision, spoke negatively about Christians who are critical of Clinton. The group also included Richard Mouw, the president of Fuller Theological Seminary, and Philip Yancey.

Rich Lowry writes, "Are these folks getting snookered by Clinton's spiritual avowals?" and then notes how difficult it can be to distinguish the personal Clinton from the politician. What is clear, Lowry continues, "is that some evangelicals are innocent of the political import of their Clinton praise."[33]

According to James Smith of the Christian Life Commission of the Southern Baptist Convention, the Clinton White House wants "the evangelical leaders to go out of the meetings and tell the media and tell their friends, 'You know, I think he is seriously devoted to his faith.'"[34] And what are the evangelicals receiving in exchange for the propaganda value of their endorsements? Little more than "bones and thin gruel," says Larry Sabata, a political science professor at the University of Virginia. According to Sabata, Clinton "must be really chuckling over this."[35]

CLINTON AND FOUNDRY UNITED METHODIST CHURCH

While it may be impossible at this time to know where Clinton's spiritual interests really lie, it is hardly irrelevant that he and his family now attend one of Washington's most liberal churches. Coincidentally, after the new pastor, J. Philip Wogaman, assumed leadership of the Foundry United Methodist Church, Senator and Mrs. Robert Dole announced that they would no longer attend the church because of its liberalism.[36]

In April 1995, Cal Thomas's nationally syndicated column included comments about Pastor Wogaman's far-left political views, which the minister regards as a sign of his kinship with the biblical prophets. Somewhat less in step with Scripture, Thomas noted, are Wogaman's publicly stated doubts about such essential Christian beliefs as the Virgin Birth and the authority of the Bible. According to Thomas, Wogaman has compared critics of his liberal views to the people responsible for the Oklahoma City bombing.

Symptomatic of Wogaman's style was a homosexuality symposium held at the church on November 10, 1995. The event, called "Sharing Our Rainbow of Light," was organized by PFLAG ("Parents, Families and Friends of Lesbians and Gays"). Mark Tooley, a United Methodist clergyman who also works for the Institute of Religion and Democracy, has described portions of the symposium that "featured ridicule of the Christmas Nativity story, speculation about Jesus as a 'drag queen,' praise for homosexual marriage, and a declaration that the Ten Commandments are 'immoral.'"[37]

The keynote speaker at the symposium, Episcopal Bishop John Spong, is well-known for his repudiation of distinctive Christian beliefs. Bishop Spong shocked even members of his liberal audience by denying that Old Testament prophecies literally foretold the coming of Christ. Tooley reports how a homosexual member of the audience protested by saying, "I am a gay, Jewish Christian, convicted by the biblical prophecies and in my heart." He then asked Bishop Spong, "Don't the Hebrew Scriptures point in the direction of Jesus?" Spong's answer was no. Spong also claimed that Paul was a homosexual, leading him to add, "Our primary understanding of God's grace came from a self-hating, gay man."

During the service, Tooley notes, "The Reverend Kwabena Rainey Cheeks of the Inner Light Unity Fellowship, a New Age group, prayed to 'ancestors, lights, angels, saints and the spirits of Buddha, Mohammed, and Jesus.'"

Pastor Wogaman reported being stimulated by Bishop Spong's remarks: "I'm not sure what to do with Bishop Spong's thoughts on St. Paul being gay. But I am much touched by the relationships of gay couples in this church." Wogaman added his opinion that King David may have been bisexual.

In another publication, Tooley reports that while there are 37,000 United Methodist Churches in the United States, only 87 of them have officially rejected Methodism's disapproval of homosexual practices. Foundry United Methodist Church is one of the 87.[38]

Given the evangelical Left's distress over the political activism of conservative Christians, it is worth noting the way Wogaman uses his pulpit and his church to propagate his liberal politics. During one service attended by both the Clinton and Dole families, Wogaman distributed anti-Republican material in the church's social hall.[39] Wogaman's preferred method for helping the poor is programs of the liberal welfare state. In 1992 Wogaman stated that America's free markets "must not prevent us from using aspects of socialism."[40] In 1967 he stated that "It is highly questionable whether Christians in Russia or China are treated any worse than Marxists in the United States."[41]

When President Clinton chooses to profess certain moral and religious convictions to evangelicals, they have a duty to check those claims against the beliefs and practices of his chosen place of worship. In neither philosophy, science, politics, nor religion is inconsistency a virtue. But none of this information seems to trouble the evangelical Left. Their silence in the face of these matters removes them from the company of the biblical prophets they so often claim as predecessors.

Chapter Twelve

For Crying Out Loud

The time has come to review *The Cry for Renewal,* released in mid-1995. Leaders of the evangelical Left have acted for several months as though the future of their movement hinges on the success of this document and their promised activities during the 1996 political campaign.[1] Many careful readers have found the document misleading and disappointing. In the last half of the chapter, therefore, I reproduce a much more promising statement that a group of forty evangelicals put together in the spring of 1987. While *The Cry for Renewal* is almost totally silent about biblical and theological issues, the other document, *The Villars Statement on Relief and Development,* addresses the issue of worldwide poverty and related matters within the context of a biblically informed worldview.

THE CRY FOR RENEWAL

On May 23, 1995, Jim Wallis, Ron Sider, Tony Campolo, and several other representatives of the evangelical Left met with a small group of reporters at the National Press Club in Washington, D.C. They were there to distribute copies and do public relations work on behalf of a Wallis-authored document titled *The Cry for Renewal.* The purpose of the document, Wallis says, is to send "a clear message to the nation's media and political leaders: Let other voices be heard."[2] Following the press conference, the group retired to Capitol Hill for visits with several leaders of Congress with the aim of, in Wallis's words, correcting "the public impression of a monolithic right-wing evangelical jugernaut."[3] Their agenda, however, really amounted to a reiteration of complaints they have leveled against evangelical conservatives since the early seventies. What made the resuscitation of their old message necessary in 1995 were the 1994 congressional elections, which saw Republicans gain control of the House of Representatives for the first time in more than forty years, and the success of such conservative Christian organizations as the Christian Coalition.

According to Wallis, *The Cry for Renewal* has been signed by "more than 100 Christian leaders from a diversity of traditions,"[4] some of them militantly anti-evangelical. Even more important to Wallis was the publicity he and his colleagues garnered in newspapers and television spots across the nation.[5]

Many people think *The Cry for Renewal* is the product of long and intense dialogue among a team of experts, but according to Michael Cromartie of the Ethics and Public Policy Center, Wallis was the major author, with some possible revisions by Tony Campolo. Most of the people who signed the document did not participate in its formulation; they were simply sent the document and invited to sign it. Some of them, I suspect, either did not read the document very carefully or interpreted it differently from the way Wallis very likely intended it.[6]

The document begins with the evangelical Left's obligatory attack on conservatives and its perfunctory criticism of liberals. It then says, "We are Evangelical voices who seek a biblical approach to politics, not an ideological agenda."[7] This is an old trick that the evangelical Left has used for two decades: Claim the high ground (the Bible) for your own cause and accuse the Christians you oppose of grubby, ideologically motivated politics. Some of the evangelical signers of the document, I suspect, would have repudiated the nasty triumphalism of this claim, had they recognized it, but sometimes it is difficult to catch subtle nuances in written communications. It is worth noting that the language in the document at this point appears to conflict with Ron Sider's more conciliatory statements over the past few years.

Further, the document declares that "inflamed rhetoric and name calling is no substitute for real and prayerful dialogue between different constituencies.... We challenge any political litmus test that distorts the independent moral conscience that faith can bring to politics.... We are dismayed by those who would undermine the integrity of religious conviction that does not conform to a narrow ideological agenda." Ironically, the very complaints the document directs against conservatives describe the way the evangelical Left has behaved for years.

The signers "are deeply concerned about the subversion of prophetic religion when wealth and power are extolled rather than held accountable, and when the gospel mesage is turned upside down to bring more comfort to those on the top of society than to those at the bottom." This is an oversimplified distortion of the relevant economic issues.

Continuing the attack on Christian conservatives, the document states, "The almost total identification of the Religious Right with the New Republican majority in Washington is a dangerous liaison of religion with political power. With the ascendancy and influence of the Christian Right in party circles, the religious critique of power has been replaced with the religious competition for power." This outrageous accusation was answered recently by Robert Dugan, vice president in charge of the Office of Public Affairs of the National Association of Evangelicals (NAE) in Washington, D.C. Whenever Dugan is asked why evangelicals so frequently align themselves with the Republican Party, he answers that it is usually the other way around:

> The Republican party aligns itself with evangelicals because ... evangelicals are more conservative, generally, than are most other segments of the population. Republicans have been actively cultivating evangelicals, and the Republican party was a natural place for them to end up.
>
> The Nationals Association of Evangelicals (NAE) was asked in 1984 if it would like to testify before the Republican party's platform committee. We accepted. We made plans months in advance and testified, but we also took the initiative and went to the Democrats when we realized that

the Democrats were not going to come to us for their platform committee.

In response to our overture, a Democratic staffer told
us that the Democratic party was not going to have such
hearings. He lied. The Democratic party platform commitee
held public hearings in Kansas City on May 31 [1984] and
in Columbus, Ohio, four days later. The National Abortion
Rights Action League (NARAL) was invited, but the NAE
was not. I asked if we could submit written testimony. The
staffer who responded said, with clear boredom in his voice,
"Yes, well, if you get testimony in to us." . . . They did not
even pretend to be interested.

You have a party, then, with a gay and lesbian caucus
since 1984, that at least unofficially has antagonized evangelicals. You have another party that has cultivated evangelicals and tailored its platform to suit our moral concerns.
Given this state of affairs, it is not surprising that evangelicals identify more with Republicans.[8]

Dugan concluded his remarks by saying, "The NAE is not part
of a particular political organization. We can't be, and we are not.
Our people are in both parties. We are anxious to have our input
anywhere we can."

The Cry for Renewal then turns in the other direction: "Like-
wise, the continuing close identification of religious liberalism with
political liberalism and the Democratic Party has demonstrated a
public witness often lacking in moral imagination or prophetic
integrity. Liberal religious leaders have sought access and influence
with those in power no less than their Religious Right counterparts."
This criticism of mainline Protestant liberals is well-taken, of course,
but it is hard to see why this last sentence is not also an implicit criticism of Tony Campolo and other liberals who respond eagerly to
White House initiatives, as we observed in chapter 11.

The statement continues, "We refuse the false choices between
personal responsibility or social justice, between good values or good
jobs, between strong families or strong neighborhoods, between sexual morality or civil rights for homosexuals, between the sacredness

of life or the rights of women, between fighting cultural corrosion or battling racism." Assuming that "the rights of women" includes the right to abortion on demand, one must wonder if Ron Sider was paying attention when he signed on to this point. Moreover, responsible conservatives do not oppose the civil rights of homosexuals; it is the rest of the homosexual agenda that is the problem.

The document concludes by saying, "We will join with anyone in the search for new solutions rooted in local communities, moral values, and social responsibility." There is plenty of room for skepticism.

A survey of the those who signed the document reveals the names of many people I admire, including several friends of mine. But the names also include a number of people who are unsympathetic—in some cases, even contemptuous—toward evangelical belief and practice: Joan Brown Campbell, General Secretary of the National Council of Churches; Marie Dennis of Maryknoll Justice and Peace,[9] Dr. James Forbes, pastor of Riverside Church in New York City; Roman Catholic cleric J. Bryan Hehir; the Rev. Dr. Paul Sherry, president of the United Church of Christ denomination; and the Rt. Rev. Edmond L. Browning of the Episcopal Church. How can the document be portrayed as "evangelical" with signers like these?

Many other signers of *The Cry for Renewal* have been long-time supporters of the evangelical Left: Sider; Campolo; Tom Sine; William Dyrness and William Pannell of Fuller Theological Seminary; author Richard Foster; Howard Snyder of the United Theological Seminary; Eldin Villafane of Gordon-Conwell Theological Seminary; Gordon MacDonald, past president of InterVarsity Christian Fellowship; and three college presidents, Roberta Hestenes of Eastern College, Daniel Chamberlain of Houghton College, and Jay Kesler of Taylor University. For the record, I believe that many of the evangelical signers would have had no difficulty signing the second document covered in this chapter.

Three published statements criticizing *The Cry for Renewal* are worthy of mention:

First, James Skillen, executive director of the Center for Public Justice, an organization with no ties to the Christian Right, has described it as "a reactionary document, a plea to be heard and get attention by people who fear that—because of the Christian Coalition's newly achieved clout—they are no longer viewed as significant voices in the public dialogue."[10]

Second, Diane Knippers, president of the Institute on Religion and Democracy, has stated, "The Religious Left's rhetoric against the Republican agenda is no less a liaison of religion with political power than the Religious Right's support for it."[11]

Third, Richard John Neuhaus, the Roman Catholic editor-in-chief of *First Things*, focuses on the same statements as Knippers. While Neuhaus agrees about the dangers of alliances between religion and political power, he points out that "it seems somewhat late, if not disingenuous, for some of the signers to be pointing that out." He explains, "Jim Wallis, Presiding Bishop Edmond Browning of the Episcopal Church, and Joan Campbell Brown of the National Council of Churches (NCC) have devoted most of their lives to cultivating the liaison between religion and liberal politics."[12] While the document insists that it speaks for "biblical faith," Neuhaus notes that it defines this faith

> exclusively in terms moral, social, and political. In this curious version of "biblical faith", there is not a mention of sin, redemption, the cross, resurrection, or the hope of glory. We counted one reference to God and one to Jesus, the latter only to point out that he teaches us not "to abandon or blame the poor for their oppression." We are told that "religious faith and values" should make public discourse "more honest, moral, civil, and spiritually sensitive."[13]

Neuhaus observes that the document fails to mention abortion, euthanasia, parental choice in education, religion in the public schools, dependency on welfare, crime, and the collapse of essential family structures. In his view, *The Cry for Renewal* amounts to "a patently partisan attack on the 'dangerous liaison of religion with political power' by those whose party used to be in charge of that liaison." The document refuses "to address the issues that most divide Americans, it exacerbates the incivility that it deplores, and it has little or nothing to do with biblical faith."[14] According to Michael Cromartie, the evangelical leftists behind *The Cry for Renewal* are simply trying to reenergize their careers on the back of the Christian Coalition.

People uninformed about the true nature of conservatism and liberalism feel good when they can sign a statement that concerns poverty and justice. It is difficult to understand their enthusiasm when it turns out that the document says almost nothing about the causes and solutions for such social ills. Ironically, the people who wrote the document have supported the very social policies and programs that have produced the conditions they now seek to ease. One would have wished for a better document than *The Cry for Renewal*. As it turns out, one example of such a document, though not as well-known, has been around since 1987, as we shall see.

AND NOW THE REST OF THE STORY

The Cry for Renewal leadership, under its new name "The Call to Renewal," sponsored a conference in Washington, D.C., in February 1996. The conference unwittingly clarified the fact that centrism and moderation are not part of Jim Wallis's intentions for the movement. It also supported the contention made earlier in this chapter that many of the responsible evangelicals who signed *The Cry for Renewal* document in 1995 may have misunderstood the real agenda behind it.

In a report in *Christianity Today,* Ted Olsen notes that while the Call to Renewal leadership continues to claim to be a group of centrists criticizing both Right and Left, the February conference "largely ignored ... shortcomings of the Left."[15] Given the number of times the Religious Left is quoted in this book as deploring the Christian conservatives' occasional use of voter guides, it is ironic that the Call to Renewal organization has announced its intention to create and distribute a guide of its own.[16]

According to Mark Tooley of the Institute for Religion and Democracy, an observer at the conference, the vast majority of participants were well-known partisans of politically liberal causes, including a surprisingly large number of people generally thought to be anti-evangelical. *Christianity Today* reports a split within the organization. When Ron Sider spoke on behalf of his opposition to abortion, a number of people in the audience expressed their disapproval.[17] Similar disagreement met Sider's argument that the Call to Renewal should support heterosexuality as the appropriate social standard. According to *Christianity Today*, one homosexual in the audience, an American Baptist pastor, walked out of the meeting after Sider's remarks.[18]

Tooley reports that a split has developed between Wallis and Tony Campolo on one side and Ron Sider on the other. In Tooley's words, "Ron Sider's insistence on upholding traditional Christian stances on homosexuality and abortion seems to have upset Campolo and Wallis. There is great dissatisfaction at ESA [Evangelicals for Social Action, of which Sider is president] over the Call to Renewal Conference[19] and its extreme leftward drift." According to Tooley, a number of people at ESA believe that "most evangelicals who signed the original Cry for Renewal statement did so only because of ESA's encouragement, and that Wallis could not have done so alone."[20]

Tooley's comments seem to be supported by ESA staff quoted in *Christianity Today*. Dwight Ozard, who edits ESA's *Prism* magazine, is quoted as saying, "There are about fifteen competing agendas, and the reason they're competing is because the thing that drew them together is a vague, nebulous call to 'renewing the nation' and 'renewing the church,' all of which sound really good but have no content." Another ESA staff person, Keith Pavlischek, concurred when he declared, "This is unlikely to go anywhere unless they make a very clear statement on the sanctity of [unborn] human life and a clear statement on Christian marriage [the homosexual issue]. The equivocation by some key leaders in the Call on these issues is a call for concern." While *Christianity Today* does not identify the key leaders exhibiting this alleged "equivocation," it would seem to point to both Jim Wallis and Tony Campolo.

The coordinator for the February conference was the Sojourners' national organizer, Duane Shank, whose ties to far

Left organizations is detailed in a report issued by the Malden Institute. The report states:

> In the 1970s and early 1980s, Shank was director of the antimilitary [National] Committee Against Registration and the Draft (CARD). In that capacity, in November 1979, he was a workshop leader at the founding conference of the U.S. Peace Council (USPC), the U.S. affiliate of the Moscow-controlled World Peace Council.... In May 1981, he was an endorser of a march on the Pentagon against U.S. efforts to keep the Castroite guerrillas in El Salvador from seizing power as the Sandinistas had just done in Nicaragua. Shank's opposition to the U.S. military did not extend to the supporters of Marxist and anti-U.S. terrorists.[21]

One of the many things that point to the political bias of the group behind the February conference was the number of participants having strong ties to the Clintons. Almost all the mainline church leaders present at the conference have made their support for the incumbent President and the Democratic party abundantly clear. One of the speakers, Michael Lerner, was widely identified in 1993 as Hillary Rodham Clinton's New Age guru. Lerner's speech used his description for his own movement, "the politics of meaning," as a way of expressing his approval of the Call to Renewal Conference.

Lerner invited those at the Call to Renewal Conference to attend a conference he had organized for April 1996, where such well-known theological liberals as Harvey Cox and the Reverend Jesse Jackson, Jr., were scheduled to speak. Also on the program in April were Jim Wallis and Rabbi Arthur Wasdow, who had worked for the Institute of Policy Studies in the 1970s. One participant was Marian Wright Edelman, the founder-president of the Children's Defense Fund and a close friend and former employer of the First Lady. Literature for Lerner's conference mentioned the similarities between his forthcoming book *The Politics of Meaning* and Jim Wallis's book *The Soul of Politics*.

It seems clear that whatever the Cry for Renewal movement was thought to be during the summer of 1995, it appears to be going in a very different direction—equivocating on crucial issues such as abortion and homosexuality—and may represent opinions far to the left of many of the signers. If this is so, it is easy to understand the discontent at ESA, especially given Ron Sider's belief that it was his reputation that led many responsible evangelicals to sign the original document. And that brings us to an examination of a very different declaration.

THE VILLARS STATEMENT ON RELIEF AND DEVELOPMENT

In late May 1987, forty evangelical Christians from around the world gathered in Villars, Switzerland, a short walk up the mountain from Francis Schaeffer's famous study center known as L'Abri. These Christians spent five days discussing and debating the subject of "Biblical Mandates for Relief and Development." What brought them together was a common concern that a growing number of Christian relief and development organizations were failing in two respects: They had lost their concern with evangelism, and they were often pursuing policies inspired by Marxist ideas. The document the group produced is called *The Villars Statement on Relief and Development.* With the permission of the Fieldstead Institute and Crossway Books, I reproduce the last two segments and the conclusion of the document.[22] There is merit in comparing the *Villars Statement*'s inclusion of biblical and theological themes with the almost total absence of these concerns from *The Cry for Renewal.*

The authors of the *Villars Statement* begin by noting thirteen failings of Christian relief and development organizations. The comments are helpful for setting criteria for any group of Christians interested in alleviating poverty and hunger:

1. The failure to operate from a distinctively Biblical perspective in both methods and goals.

2. The tendency to focus on meeting material needs without sufficient emphasis on spiritual needs.

3. The attempt to synthesize Marxist categories and Christian concepts, to equate economic liberation with salvation, and to use the Marxist critique, without recognizing the basic conflict between these views and the Biblical perspective.

4. The emphasis on redistribution of wealth as the answer to poverty and deprivation without recognizing the value of incentive, opportunity, creativity, and economic and political freedom.

5. The attraction to centrally controlled economies and coercive solutions despite the failures of such economies and their consistent violation of the rights of the poor.

6. A disproportionate emphasis on changing structures without recognizing the frequency with which this only exchanges one oppressive structure for another.

7. The danger of utopian and ideological entrapment, whether from the left or the right.

8. Neglecting to denounce oppression when it comes from one end or the other of the political spectrum.

9. Focusing on external causes of poverty in exploitation and oppression without confronting those internal causes that are rooted in patterns of belief and behavior within a given culture.[23]

10. The need to make conversion and discipleship an essential component of Christian relief and development work, and to carry this out in conjunction with the local church.

11. The need to apply the teaching of the Bible as a whole in the areas of personal life, family, and work, but equally in the shaping of the culture and social life.

12. The need to reaffirm the Biblical support for the family as the basic social and economic unit and its right to own and control property, and to stand against any ideology that would diminish the family's proper role in any of these areas.

13. The need to oppose a false understanding of poverty which makes poverty itself a virtue, or which sanctifies those who are poor on the basis of their poverty.[24]

It is worth noting that this 1987 document anticipated every worthy recommendation now promoted by the evangelical Left as part of their "newly discovered centrist way." Moreover, it also wisely repudiates the leftist sentiments that still haunt the evangelical Left's efforts to formulate an effective and biblical way of dealing with hunger, poverty, and oppression.

The statement continues by noting seven facets of biblical teaching that hold important implications for Christian efforts to deal with worldwide hunger and poverty.

1. God created mankind in His own image, endowing man with freedom, creativity, significance, and moral discernment. Moreover, prior to the Fall man lived in harmony with all of God's creation, free from pain, suffering, and death.

2. The devastating reality of sin and evil (hunger, oppression, deprivation, disease, death, and separation from God) is the result of man's rebellion against God, which began at the Fall and continues through history.

3. The causes of hunger and deprivation, therefore, are spiritual as well as material and can only be dealt with adequately insofar as the spiritual dimension is taken into account.

4. Man's rebellion against God affects every aspect of human existence. The Fall resulted in God's curse on creation and in destructive patterns of thought, culture, and relationships, which keep men and women in bondage to poverty and deprivation.

5. The work of Christian relief and development, therefore, must involve spiritual transformation, setting people free from destructive attitudes, beliefs, values, and patterns of

culture. The proclamation of the gospel and the making of disciples, then, is an unavoidable dimension of relief and development work—not only for eternal salvation, but also for the transformation of culture and economic life.

6.   When people were held in bondage to hunger and deprivation by unjust social structures, the Bible consistently denounced those who perpetuated such oppression and demanded obedience to God's law. The Biblical emphasis, then, is not on "sinful structures" but rather on sinful human choices that perpetuate suffering and injustice.

7.   God's ultimate answer for suffering and deprivation is the gift of His only Son, Jesus Christ, who broke the power of sin and death by His own death and resurrection. The decisive victory was won on the cross in the atoning death of Christ for all who would believe Him. The final victory will be accomplished when Christ returns in power and glory to reign with His people. Until that time all who claim Jesus as their Lord are called to care for those in need as the Holy Spirit enables them to share the only message of true hope for a broken world.[25]

Here, I suggest, is a document worth signing.[26] It specifically addresses the biblical issues that Richard John Neuhaus finds missing from *The Cry for Renewal*. I suspect that many of the evangelicals who signed *The Cry for Renewal* would willingly sign the *Villars Statement*, among them Ron Sider, Tony Campolo, and Tom Sine. My confidence in this regard does not extend to Jim Wallis.

Moreover, if it came to having to choose between the two documents, I suspect that some original supporters of *The Cry for Renewal* would prefer the *Villars Statement* over Wallis's vague, incomplete, and politically motivated document. But I also know some signers of *The Cry for Renewal* who would refuse to sign the *Villars Statement*. This group would most certainly include the theological liberals who will be offended by the statement's endorsement of the Gospel message of Jesus' atoning death and resurrection.

CONCLUSION

This examination of the two documents and the Call for Renewal Conference is instructive for several reasons. First, it effectively unmasks the misinformation in the evangelical liberals' claim to have discovered a "new" and centrist way of dealing with poverty. Second, it reveals the dishonesty present in liberal assertions that evangelical conservatives lack compassion for the poor and the commitment to deal with that poverty. Finally, it demonstrates that while segments of the Left continue to downplay the importance of New Testament evangelism and biblically based theology, evangelical conservatives have found a way to be faithful to both their social responsibility and their faith. What is new in *The Cry for Renewal* doesn't ring true, and what is important in that document is not new.

Chapter Thirteen

What You Don't Know Can Hurt You (and Others, Too)

There are several reasons why a brief and simple discussion of economics belongs in this book. First, the Left's economic illiteracy is responsible for several of its more serious errors, such as its attack on capitalism. When it comes to economics, the Left simply has had no idea what it is talking about. Second, while evangelical liberals like Ron Sider and Tony Campolo have finally acknowledged the failures of socialism and have rejected it in favor of what they think is "capitalism," large numbers of religious leftists continue to carry on an infatuation with statism[1] and socialism. Third, even when evangelical liberals like Sider and Campolo are right (as with their rejection of socialism), they may be so for the wrong reasons.

Many Christians act as though the only thing that counts in the matter of helping the poor is *intention*. But when good intentions are not wedded to sound *economic* theory, they typically result in actions that produce consequences directly opposite to those that were intended. Economist Benjamin Rogge had this in mind when he wrote that

> the typical American who calls himself a Christian and who makes pronouncements on economic policies or institutions does so out of an almost complete ignorance of the

simplest and most widely accepted tools of economic analysis. If something arouses his Christian concern, he asks not whether it is water or gasoline he is tossing on the economic fire—he asks only whether it is a well-intended act. As I understand it, the Christian is required to use his God-given reason as well.[2]

As we have seen, good intentions combined with bad theory have produced bad policies that have harmed the very people they were supposed to help.

THREE ECONOMIC OPTIONS

It is a mistake to think that capitalism and socialism are the only two systems of economics from which to choose. Floating somewhere between capitalism and socialism is a third system that is the cause of much confusion. The best name for this middle system is "interventionism"—suggesting the importance it gives to a government's intervention in the operation of a market system with policies or actions that seem likely to facilitate its social goals.[3]

Evangelical author Herbert Schlossberg recognizes the difference between capitalism and interventionism as they are practiced in the United States. To the question of whether Christians should support capitalism, he replies:

> If by capitalism one means the present system of statist manipulation of resources and people for the benefit of those who run the political system and their adherents, the answer is no. If it [capitalism] means the free and responsible ownership of resources by all who give value for what they receive, without the application of coercive power, then the answer is yes.[4]

It is important to realize, Schlossberg says, that the economy of the United States is interventionist, not capitalist. Many complaints about the economic policies of the United States are justified. But when the policies that cause problems result from interventionism, it is unfair to blame those problems on capitalism.

The opponents of capitalism play an interesting game with interventionist economics. First, their criticisms of what they call "capitalism" are in fact directed at the bad economic consequences of interventionist policies; they blame capitalism for what are in fact the results of governmental intrusion into market activities. Second, once they succeed in persuading enough people that capitalism has produced some bad consequence such as a recession, inflation, or high unemployment, they then offer their "solution" for the problem. As it turns out, the "solution" is usually more of the same kind of governmental intervention that produced the bad consequence. Needless to say, this is a very clever way of advancing one's cause: blaming the economic system you despise (capitalism) for consequences resulting from the economic system (interventionism) you promote.

THE TWO MEANS OF EXCHANGE

An excellent way of getting at the essential difference between capitalism and socialism is a distinction, drawn most recently by African-American economist Walter Williams, between what he calls *the peaceful means of exchange* and *the violent means of exchange*.[5]

The peaceful means of exchange may be summed up in the phrase, "If you do something good for me, then I'll do something good for you." When capitalism is understood correctly, it epitomizes the peaceful means of exchange. The reason people enter market exchanges is because they believe the exchange is good for them. They take advantage of an opportunity to obtain something they want more in exchange for something they value less. Capitalism, then, should be understood as a voluntary system of relationships that utilizes the peaceful means of exchange.

But exchange can also take place by means of force and violence. In this violent means of exchange, the basic rule of thumb is, "Unless you do something good for me, I'll do something bad to you." This turns out to be the controlling principle of both socialism and interventionism.

Socialism means far more than centralized control of the economic process. It entails the introduction of coercion into economic exchange in order to facilitate the goals of the elite who function as the central planners. Even if we fail to notice any other contrast between capitalism and socialism, we already have a major difference to relate to the biblical ethic. One system stresses voluntary and peaceful exchange while the other depends on coercion and violence (implicit or explicit). Viewed another way, socialism is an economic system that replaces the market as the means of providing for consumption, production, and distribution with a system of central planning. Under socialism, physical capital[6] is either owned or controlled by the state.

Some Christian socialists object to this link between socialism and coercion. They would like us to believe that a more humane, noncoercive kind of socialism is possible. They would like us to think that there is a form of socialism—not yet tried anywhere on earth—in which the central ideas are cooperation and community and from which coercion and tyranny are precluded. I contend that such people, to put it kindly, are confused.

It is interesting to note how little information Christian socialists provide about the workings of this supposedly more humane kind of socialism. "Voluntary socialism" is a contradiction in terms. What Christian socialists do is form a utopian ideal of a voluntary community and then call it socialism. They are unable to explain how their system will work without free markets, and they simply ignore the massive amounts of coercion that will be required to get their system started. Whatever else socialism is, it means a centralized control of the economy made possible by the use of force. It follows, therefore, that Acts 2:44–45—an account of how early Christians pooled their resources—does not describe some primitive type of Christian socialism. What those early believers did was voluntary. No government coerced them. Attempts to use that text in an effort to make Christians sympathetic to socialism is dishonest.

A BRIEF WORD ABOUT INTERVENTIONISM

Many people are attracted by the possibility of an economic system that would fall somewhere between capitalism and socialism, combining, they hope, the best features of each. When Ronald Sider says he has suddenly become a proponent of capitalism, what he really has in mind is an interventionist system. Interventionism results from the mistaken belief that governmental intervention in economic matters can successfully achieve desired results while still falling short of the more complete control that characterizes a socialist system.

This is what a mixed economy is *supposed* to be. In reality, it turns out to be a system in which government alters the terms of trade in ways that benefit some at the expense of others. Advocates of interventionism never explain this. Instead, they talk in lofty moral terms about the importance of certain social goals that can only be attained through government intervention. Supposedly, this will counter the alleged selfishness of some in order to bring about the good for all.[7]

WHY SOCIALISM CANNOT WORK

The miserable performance of socialist economies is no accident. They do not work, because they cannot work. One of the most important features of a market economy is its informational function. Rising and falling prices give astute entrepreneurs vital information about changes in supply and demand. When government intervenes in the economy—by restraining price increases, for example—it shuts off important signals that entrepreneurs might otherwise use in making economic decisions. That information is simply not available in a socialist system. Without free markets to set prices, socialists can never attune production to human wants. The impossibility of precise measures of cost accounting under socialism explains the failure of socialist systems.

As an example, suppose that I am the director of a Soviet factory that produces ten thousand widgets a day. Even though I might be a good socialist, I still want to sell every widget we make. But I have a problem, which is, knowing the price we should ask. The manager of a widget factory in a market system has a distinct advantage in determining price. Because he knows the cost of his machines, raw materials, rent, utilities, and labor, he can calculate what it costs to make each widget. But in a socialist state, the government owns everything: the land, the raw materials, the utilities, the factory, the machines, and so on. In a socialist economy, it is impossible to know the cost of the manufactured widgets; because the first requirement of a rational price is to exceed one's costs, it is impossible to know what price to charge. So as the director of a Soviet factory I have developed a novel way of setting my prices. I use spies to gather and report a steady stream of pricing information: Igor will check the Wal-Mart, and Tanya will visit the Sears store.

Socialism turns out to be a supposed system of planning that makes rational economic planning impossible. Without free markets and the vital information they supply, economic activity becomes chaotic and results in drastic inefficiencies and distortions. The great paradox of socialism is that socialists need capitalism in order to survive. Socialists have to make allowance for some free markets that provide the pricing information that alone makes rational economic activity possible; otherwise, socialist economies would have even more problems than those for which they are notorious. In practice, socialism is a gigantic fraud that attacks the market at the same time it is forced to utilize the market process.

Another reason why market systems work and socialism does not is that the former provide important incentives that are missing from the latter. As British economist Brian Griffiths explains, under socialism

> Rewards are not related to effort and commercial risk-taking, but to party membership, bureaucratic status, political fiat and corruption. As a consequence, the legitimate commercial entrepreneurial spirit is killed; for perfectly understandable reasons, people devote their resources to hacking a way through the political and bureaucratic jungle of their economies.[8]

Sociologist Peter Berger points out that "Even in the early 1970s it should not have been news that socialism is not good for economic growth and also that it shows a disturbing propensity

toward totalitarianism (with its customary accompaniment of ter-
ror)."[9] Claims by the rulers of the U.S.S.R., China, and Cuba that
their adoption of socialism reflected their commitment to justice
and equality was not simply empty rhetoric; it was hypocritical
deceit. "Put simply," Berger declares, "socialist equality is shared
poverty by serfs, coupled with the monopolization of both privilege
and power by a small (increasingly hereditary) aristocracy."[10] This
phenomenon of hereditary aristocracy showed up in every socialist state in our century. "It seems to be the intrinsic genius of
socialism to produce these modern facsimiles of feudalism," Berger
writes.[11] Gradually people are beginning to notice the absence of
one single example of a socialist state that has succeeded economically and has not become totalitarian. "We know, or should know,
that socialism is a mirage that leads nowhere except to economic
stagnation, collective poverty, and various degrees of tyranny."[12]

What must we think of the church intellectuals who told us
that socialism is the only economic system compatible with Christianity? What does such a claim reveal about their moral sensitiv-
ity to the millions who have suffered from such systems?

CAPITALISM AND CHRISTIAN MORAL CONCERNS

Capitalism is not economic anarchy. When properly defined, it
recognizes several necessary conditions for the kinds of voluntary
relationships it supports. One of these is the existence of inherent
human rights, such as the right to make decisions, the right to be
free, the right to hold property, and the right to exchange peacefully what one owns for something else.

Capitalism also presupposes a system of morality. Under capitalism, there are definite limits, moral and otherwise, to the ways in
which people can exchange. Capitalism should be viewed as a system of voluntary relationships within a framework of laws that protect people's rights against force, fraud, theft, and violations of
contracts. "Thou shalt not steal" and "Thou shalt not lie" are part of
the underlying moral constraints of the system.[13] After all, economic
exchanges can hardly be voluntary if one participant is coerced,
deceived, defrauded, or robbed.

Deviations from the market ideal usually occur because of defects in human nature. Human beings naturally crave security and guaranteed success, values not found readily in a free market. Genuine competition always carries with it the possibility of failure and loss. Consequently, the human desire for security leads people to avoid competition whenever possible, encourages them to operate outside the market, and induces them to subvert the market process through behavior that is often questionable and dishonest. This quest for guaranteed success often leads people to seek special favors from powerful members of government through such means as regulations and restrictions on free exchange.

One of the more effective ways of mitigating the effects of human sin in society is dispersing and decentralizing power. The combination of a free market economy and limited constitutional government is the most effective means yet devised to impede the concentration of economic and political power in the hands of a small number of people. The Religious Left should be aware that their opposition to amassing wealth and power is far more likely to bear fruit with a conservative understanding of economics and government than with the big-government approach of political liberalism.

Every person's ultimate protection against coercion requires control over some private spheres of life where he or she can be free. Private ownership of property is an important buffer against the exorbitant consolidation of power by government.

Liberal critics also contend that capitalism encourages the development of monopolies. The real source of monopolies, however, is not the free market but governmental intervention with the market.[14] The only monopolies that have ever attained lasting immunity from competition did so by governmental fiat, regulation, or support of some other kind. Governments create monopolies by granting one organization the exclusive privilege of doing business or by establishing *de facto* monopolies through regulatory agencies whose alleged purpose is the enforcement of competition but whose real effect is the limitation of competition.[15]

Economic interventionism and socialism are the real sources of monopolies. This is illustrated, for example, in the success of

the American robber barons of the nineteenth century. Without
government aid such as subsidies, the robber barons would never
have succeeded.[16]

Liberals blame capitalism for every evil in contemporary society, including its greed, materialism, selfishness, the prevalence
of fradulent behavior,[17] the debasement of society's tastes, the pollution of the environment,[18] the alienation and despair within
society,[19] and vast disparities of wealth.[20] Even racism and sexism
are treated as effects of capitalism.

Many of the objections to a market system result from a
simple but fallacious two-step operation. First, some undesirable
feature is noted in a society that is allegedly capitalistic; then it
is simply asserted that capitalism is the cause of this problem.
Logic texts call this the Fallacy of False Cause. Mere coincidence
does not prove causal connection. Moreover, this belief ignores
the fact that these same features exist in interventionist and
socialist societies.

The Issue of Greed

Liberal critics of capitalism often attack it for encouraging
greed. The truth, however, is that the mechanism of the market
actually *neutralizes* greed as it forces people to find ways of serving the needs of those with whom they wish to exchange. As long
as our rights are protected (a basic precondition of market
exchanges), the greed of others cannot harm us. As long as greedy
people are prohibited from introducing force, fraud, and theft into
the exchange process and as long as these persons cannot secure
special privileges from the state under interventionist or socialist
arrangements, their greed must be channeled into the discovery
of products or services for which people are willing to trade. Every
person in a market economy has to be other-directed. The market
is one area of life where concern for the other person is required.
The market, therefore, does not pander to greed. Rather, it is a
mechanism that allows natural human desires to be satisfied in
nonviolent ways.

Does Capitalism Exploit People?

Capitalism is also attacked on the ground that it leads to situations in which some people (the "exploiters") win at the expense of other people (the "losers"). A fancier way to put this is to say that market exchanges are examples of what is called a *zero-sum game,* namely, an exchange where only one participant can win. If one person (or group) wins, then the other must lose. Baseball and basketball are two examples of zero-sum games. If A wins, then B must lose.

The error here consists in thinking that market exchanges are a zero-sum game. On the contrary, market exchanges illustrate what is called a *positive-sum* game, that is, one in which both players may win. We must reject the myth that economic exchanges necessarily benefit only one party at the expense of the other. In voluntary economic exchanges, both parties may leave the exchange in better economic shape than would otherwise have been the case. To repeat the message of the peaceful means of exchange, "If you do something good for me, then I will do something good for you." If both parties did not believe they gained through the trade, if each did not see the exchange as beneficial, they would not continue to take part in it.

CONCLUSION

Most religious critics of capitalism focus their attacks on what they take to be its moral shortcomings. In truth, the moral objections to capitalism turn out to be a sorry collection of claims that reflect, more than anything else, serious confusions about the real nature of a market system. When capitalism is put to the moral test, it beats its competition easily. Among all of our economic options, Arthur Shenfield writes, only capitalism

> operates on the basis of respect for free, independent, responsible persons. All other systems in varying degrees treat men as less than this. Socialist systems above all treat

men as pawns to be moved about by the authorities, or as children to be given what the rulers decide is good for them, or as serfs or slaves. The rulers begin by boasting about their compassion, which in any case is fraudulent, but after a time they drop this pretense which they find unnecessary for the maintenance of power. In all things they act on the presumption that they know best. Therefore they and their systems are morally stunted. Only the free system, the much assailed capitalism, is morally mature.[21]

The alternative to free exchange is coercion and violence. Capitalism is a mechanism that allows natural human desires to be satisfied in a nonviolent way. Little can be done to prevent people from wanting to be rich, Shenfield says. That's the way things often are in a fallen world. But what capitalism does is channel that desire into peaceful means that benefit many besides those who wish to improve their own situation in life. "The alternative to serving other men's wants," Shenfield concludes, "is seizing power of them, as it always has been. Hence it is not surprising that wherever the enemies of capitalism have prevailed, the result has been not only the debasement of consumption standards for the masses but also their reduction to serfdom by the new privileged class of Socialist rulers."[22]

Once people realize that few things in life are free, that most things carry a price tag, and that therefore we have to work for most of the things we want, we are in a position to learn a vital truth about life. Capitalism helps teach this truth. But under socialism, Arthur Shenfield warns, "Everything still has a cost, but everyone is tempted, even urged to behave as if there is no cost or as if the cost will be borne by somebody else. This is one of the most corrosive effects of collectivism upon the moral character of people."[23]

And so, we see, capitalism is not merely the more effective economic system; it is also morally superior. When capitalism, the system of free economic exchange, is described fairly, it comes closer to matching the demands of the biblical ethic than does either socialism or interventionism.

These are the real reasons why Ron Sider and his friends in the Religious Left should have abandoned the statist economic policies they promoted in the past. These are also the reasons why they should now end their advocacy of economic interventionism, which only encourages the consolidation of wealth and power in the hands of the few. Christians who are sincere about wanting to help the poor should support the market system described in this chapter.

Chapter Fourteen

Will the Real Friends of the Poor Please Stand Up?

Tony Campolo and Ron Sider have recently admitted something that conservatives have been saying for years, namely, that the liberal welfare state has caused enormous harm to large numbers of America's poor. When conservatives used to make this claim, they were dismissed as heartless, uncaring, cruel purveyors of injustice.

THE EXTENT OF AMERICA'S ASSISTANCE TO THE POOR

Since at least 1982, an amazing statistic about the extent of America's aid to the poor has gone largely unnoticed. Less than 25 percent of all the tax dollars allocated to fight poverty at every level of government reaches the poor. The other 75 percent goes to pay for overhead.[1] Clearly, the bucket used to carry money from the pockets of the taxpayer to the poor is leaking badly.

As African-American economist Thomas Sowell notes, this means that most of the tax dollars collected to fight poverty end up "in the pockets of highly paid administrators, consultants, and staff as well as higher-income recipients of benefits from programs advertised as anti-poverty efforts."[2] America could raise every poor person in the country to the poverty boundary in one week and reduce the budget for the programs by 75 percent simply by eliminating the huge bureaucracy that stands between the poor and the federal treasury.

The United States is spending more than enough to fight poverty, but it has not spent that money very wisely. In the words of economists James Gwartney and Thomas McCaleb, "The problem of poverty continues to fester not because we are failing to do enough, but rather because we are doing so much that is counterproductive."[3]

HAVE ANTIPOVERTY PROGRAMS HURT THE POOR?

Much more is at stake than the enormous waste of resources. A number of recent studies have shown how well-intended but economically unsound governmental policies have caused poverty to become more entrenched in our society. These studies document how the very War on Poverty programs that were supposed to end poverty have, in fact, made worse the plight of the poor. During the mid–1980s, twenty years after the start of the War on Poverty programs, scholars had compiled enough data to show what was happening. Yet, a full decade later, they are still trying to get congressional liberals to look at this information.

It is easy to forget that before the War on Poverty began in the mid-1960s, people at the bottom of the economic ladder were making rapid strides toward improving their situation. Between 1950 and 1965, the percentage of poor Americans was cut in half (from about 30 percent to less than 15 percent). This remarkable decline took place during the fifteen years prior to the start of the War on Poverty. Poverty in America fell most rapidly during the Eisenhower-Kennedy years (1953–63), when welfare assistance was only a fraction of what it became during the 1970s and 1980s.[4]

The most rapid growth of poverty programs began, then, about the time when poverty in the United States had reached its lowest level.[5] This decline occurred without any help from any Great Society programs. The common wisdom in the mid-1960s was that the massive aid that started flowing under the War on Poverty programs would continue the reduction in poverty. But just the opposite happened. Soon after huge increases in tax transfers began, the progress against poverty slowed, then stopped, and then went into reverse. As Charles Murray documents in his book *Losing Ground: American Social Policy 1950–1980,* progress in reducing poverty stopped abruptly at the very time when federal spending on social-welfare programs began to climb astronomically.[6]

While poverty had declined from 1947 to 1968, it stood in 1980 at the same percentage as 1968 even though social-welfare spending had multiplied 400 percent during those twelve years. But the constancy of that percentage belies some important facts. While the poverty rate for people over the age of sixty-five declined during the 1970s, the rate for families under the age of twenty-five doubled from 13.2 percent in 1968 to 26.1 percent in 1982.

In the three decades since the advent of the War on Poverty programs, the United States government has spent, in all, close to five trillion dollars to end poverty. The total bill for poverty programs continued to climb during the Reagan presidency,[7] and the increases continued under Presidents Bush and Clinton. Yet the poor today suffer from less education, higher illegitimacy rates, and more unemployment—all traceable to the very programs that were supposed to improve their lot. The quality of life among America's poor is far worse today than before the War on Poverty began; the likelihood of their escaping from the poverty trap is much less.

Selected statistics reveal the magnitude of rapidly increasing welfare costs. According to official government sources, the number of food-stamp recipients was

9,083,000 in 1980,
16,254,000 in 1990,
19,471,000 in 1991, and
23,233,000 in 1992.[8]

In 1994, the government's expenditures on food stamps was $25.5 billion.[9] Total U.S. expenditures on social welfare amounted to

$303.2 billion in 1980,
$616.6 billion in 1990,
$676.4 billion in 1991, and
$749.4 billion in 1992.[10]

These numbers hardly suggest that we are winning the war against poverty.

In the view of Charles Murray, what our nation did in the name of humanitarianism was to create a system that has institutionalized poverty and entrapped millions who, along with their children, may never be able to escape. While our goal was to give the poor more, what we really did was create more poor.[11]

James Gwartney relates the failure of poverty programs to the political concerns of the Christian Left:

> Seeking to promote the welfare of the poor, the disadvantaged, the unemployed, and the misfortunate, well-meaning citizens (including a good many evangelical Christians) have inadvertently supported forms of economic organization that have promoted the precise outcomes they sought to alleviate. For too long socially concerned Christians have measured policies by the intentions of their advocates, rather than the predictable effectiveness of the programs. Put simply, in our haste to do something constructive, we have not thought very seriously about the impact, particularly in the long-run, of alternative policies on the well-being of the intended beneficiaries.[12]

THE IMPORTANCE OF INCENTIVES

One vital lesson people can learn from economics is the importance of incentives. As the expected benefits from some choice increase, the number of people choosing that option usually increases. As the anticipated costs of an action increase, the number of people choosing it usually decreases. This simple principle has somehow escaped liberals.

If we understand what makes human beings tick, we can make general predictions as to how individuals or groups will respond to new incentives. If a society establishes programs that provide unemployed people with cash and noncash benefits[13] that approximate or even exceed what they would earn working (after taxes), one can safely predict that many of these people will choose to remain unemployed. If a welfare program is set up in such a way that it provides incentives for unmarried women who become pregnant to remain unmarried, we should not be surprised when the rate of illegitimate births begins to increase. In economics, you get what you pay for.

THE HARM DONE TO AFRICAN-AMERICANS

The harm done by poverty programs to America's poor has been especially hard on African-Americans. One event that helped to focus the nation's attention on the crisis of the black family was the CBS documentary "The Vanishing Family," by Bill Moyers, that aired on January 25, 1986. Even in 1986, 60 percent of all black births were illegitimate. The actual percentage of illegitimate births in America's inner cities was much higher. Fifty percent of all black teenaged females became pregnant. In 1986, close to 50 percent of all black children were supported to some extent by some level of government. All of these numbers have increased significantly in the last decade.

As the black family continues to disintegrate, the surrounding society falls into moral chaos. More black males are murdered in America each year than the total number of blacks who died during the entire Vietnam War.

What has the crisis of the black family got to do with America's poverty programs? Glenn C. Loury, a black professor of political economy at Boston University, gives the answer. He writes, "I am persuaded by the argument of George Gilder and Charles Murray that the easy availability of fiancial support for women with children without fathers present has helped create a climate in which the breakdown in the family could be accelerated."[14] Robert Woodson, another prominent African-American and the president of the National Association of Neighborhood Enterprises, also sees the welfare state implicated in the crisis of the black family.[15] Black author Joseph Perkins declares:

> I lay the blame for the disintegration of inner-city families wholly on the welfare state. What we have is a welfare

system which creates incentives to dissolve existing family unions. . . . I think it is difficult for anyone to argue that the burgeoning welfare state did not bring about the dissolution of black families. Essentially, the state has supplanted the family among disadvantaged blacks. Young black mothers turn to the paternalistic federal government for support instead of looking to the fathers of their children. And young black males eschew their social and moral responsibilities because they too know that the state will act as their surrogate. Because of the multiplier effect, we have increasing numbers of black children born into single-parent households. And with so many children growing up in female-headed households, the importance of a husband-wife household is inevitably devalued. Thus, marriage doesn't hold the lustre among black youth in today's inner city that it did for their pre-welfare state counterparts.[16]

In even stronger terms, Warren T. Brookes laments that nothing "can begin to match the systematic degradation, dehumanization, and cultural genocide that has been wreaked on black Americans." The American government, he states, has, in the past thirty years, with the best of intentions, "seduced blacks out of the rigors of the marketplace and into the stifling womb of the welfare state."[17]

Liberal politicians, their supporters in the media, and many churches have sought to assure us that the programs of the welfare state flowed from noble objectives: They wanted to help the poor. But we have already shown that the result of the poverty programs has been entirely the opposite. While the politics and economics of the Left are justified in the name of compassion, they are speeding us headlong toward to the destruction of the black family and the disintegration of society. And this is the case even though members of the Religious Left have repeatedly assured us that what the Bible demands is more of this "humanitarian" statism.

IS WELFARE GOOD FOR CHILDREN?

In a recent report from the Heritage Foundation in Washington, D.C., Robert Rector discloses the mountain of evidence that undermines many liberal assumptions about welfare.[18] The first liberal assumption Rector's evidence challenges is the belief that the well-being and success of children increase as their family's incomes rise. This assumption is crucial to the liberal theory that such social ills as crime, school dropout, weak cognitive skills, illegitimacy, drug use, and a poor work ethic are caused by poverty. Rector answers:

> History refutes this belief. In 1950, nearly a third of the American population was poor (twice the current rate). In the 1920s, roughly half of the population was poor by today's standard. If the theory that "poverty" causes social problems were true, we should have had far more social problems in those earlier periods than we do today. But crime and most other social problems have increased rather than fallen since these earlier periods.[19]

Rector argues that the values and abilities of families are the major contributor to children's success, not the size of the family's paycheck. Efforts to increase family income through welfare not only do little to benefit children but tend to undermine the very values that are basic to children's future success.

Rector then challenges the liberal belief that welfare is a sound way to raise family income:

> Because welfare reduces work effort and promotes illegitimacy and poverty-prone single parent families, it actually may cause an overall decrease in family incomes. Welfare is extremely efficient at replacing self-sufficiency with dependence, but relatively ineffective in raising incomes and eliminating poverty.[20]

The third liberal premise that Rector disputes is the claim that welfare is good for children. In his words, "The conventional liberal assumption is that children on welfare in states with lower benefit levels will be markedly worse off than children in states with higher benefits. Children on AFDC [Aid for Dependent Children] in high benefit states . . . should have improved cognitive abilities when compared to children without access to more generous welfare."[21] Rector cites recently published research that refutes this theory. Higher welfare benefits, he reports, "did not improve children's cognitive performance."[22] The research also shows that "a 50 percent increase in monthly AFDC and food-stamp benefit levels will lead to a 75 percent increase in the number of mothers with children enrolling in AFDC and a 75 percent increase in the number of years spent on welfare."[23]

Other data from the research reveal that the longer a child stays on welfare, the lower that child's IQ is likely to be. What is damaging poor children, the evidence shows, is not poverty but welfare.[24]

CONCLUSION

Liberals love to portray themselves as the friends of the poor and paint conservatives as the enemies of the poor. When we turn away from liberal propaganda and examine the evidence, however, we discover that with friends like America's liberals, the poor do not need any enemies.

Chapter Fifteen

Love Your Enemies (Even If They Are Conservatives)

Experts estimate that the total number of evangelicals in America is somewhere around fifty million people, in the same neighborhood as the headcount for mainline denominations. At last count, the Christian Coalition had a membership of 1.7 million people, a growing number of whom are Roman Catholics and Jews.[1] That leaves approximately 49 million evangelicals who are not members. The Coalition currently has 1,700 chapters in the fifty states, and its annual budget is $25 million.

THE CLASH OF CULTURES

The widespread fear and distrust of evangelical conservatives, including the Christian Coalition, is an interesting subject. To some extent, it reflects the serious culture clash in America that has been heating up in recent years. One rather humorous example of this culture clash appeared recently in the "This Week" column of *National Review*:

> Meanwhile, the American Association of University Women [AAUW] has released a report entitled "Unmasking Religious Right Extremism," but the extremism unmasked is chiefly its own. The report includes a list of phrases that are "tipoffs

to possible religious extremist affiliation," such as: *back to basics in education, decency,*[2] *pro-family, traditional family values, moral rebirth, school choice, excellence in education,*[3] *parental control.* The report helpfully adds, "While use of these buzzwords does not prove the speaker is an extremist, it does warrant further investigation and questioning."[4]

Far less humorous are Gary Bauer's comments about the present state of the culture war. Bauer, president of the Family Research Council, chronicles the disillusionment that many Americans have with the old, liberal-dominated Washington:

> You believe that government is a limited instrument. Washington, D.C. believes that government can create a utopia on earth.
>
> You believe in a thing called "truth." Washington, D.C. believes in the all-importance of moral relativism.
>
> You believe in the importance of faith, community, and family. Washington, D.C. believes in the all-importance of the state and the "new world order."
>
> You believe that America could once more be the shining "city upon a hill" that its first settlers strove to build. Washington, D.C. believes that *it* is that city.
>
> You have watched ... how the men and women who produce the goods and services we all benefit so tremendously from have been branded as "greedy capitalists" because they have dared to succeed. These are the individuals who have driven the economic machine that makes possible all the grand schemes of Washington bureaucrats, but they have been condemned nonetheless.
>
> You have watched while the Boy Scouts of America— of all people!—have been treated like criminals. You see, the Boy Scouts are stubborn as well as backward. They still insist on following all sorts of outmoded practices, like using the word "God" in their oath of allegiance and refusing to allow homosexuals to serve in leadership positions.... President Clinton has punished them by refusing

to address their annual jamboree (the first time a sitting president has done so in this century).

You have watched while the condom (not Pepsi) has become the symbol of a new generation—a symbol deliberately and enthusiastically promoted by Washington, D.C., with your tax dollars, in the name of "sex education."[5]

It should be easy to see why people who understand all this can suddenly change from passive and inattentive Christians to social activists.

THE LIBERALS' OLD COMPLAINT

Not too long ago, religious liberals in America were busy attempting to get the federal government's help for causes and programs that they supported. Reveling in their easy access to the citadels of power, these liberals enjoyed chiding religious fundamentalists and evangelicals for their supposed indifference to social issues— for ignoring what is called the social dimension of the gospel. "All these guys ever do," the liberals pouted, "is preach what they call the gospel; they ignore everything else."[6]

Suddenly the shoe is on the other foot. Religious conservatives have discovered the social and political dimensions of the Gospel. Now the liberals wish conservatives would go back into their churches and forget the public arena.

The recent resurgence of religious conservatism in America and the determination of many people of faith to move their views and values into the forefront of public discussion is thought, by some, to pose a threat to "civil liberties, to a healthy diversity of opinion, and to the hope that we can conduct public affairs free of the divisiveness of religious factionalism."[7] As Richard John Neuhaus describes it, assorted liberal organizations believe that "the religious Right is the greatest peril to American Democracy since Joe McCarthy."[8] Of course, Neuhaus adds, the religious Right is also a financial bonanza for its critics, since nothing brings in the money more quickly than alarmist reports about the Christian Right's alleged intention to take over the country.

Thus full page advertisements in prestige newspapers inform us that the religious Right is determined to abolish the no-establishment clause of the First Amendment, impose its fundamentalist morality on all of us through law, put politicians in our bedrooms, censor what we may read and see, and then, for good measure, blow up the world in order to force history's denoument in the final act of Armaggeddon.[9]

There is no question about the fact that some people in America want the rest of us to believe these claims. But are the claims true? Do conservative Christians really want to bring about this scenario? If not, what are they actually trying to accomplish?

Neuhaus's comment about blowing up the world to force the end of history is reminiscent of Jim Wallis's attempt to link President Reagan to such views during the 1984 presidential campaign. According to Wallis, Reagan had been reading writers, like Hal Lindsey, who predicted that the imminent return of Christ in the Rapture would be followed by a time of cataclysmic destruction (the so-called Tribulation Period), after which the world would be destroyed by fire. This was supposed to explain Reagan's fascination with nuclear weapons, implying that he secretly wished to be God's agent in destroying the planet. It was also calculated to frighten uninformed voters. Wallis's critics pointed out that Wallis surely knew that the theology in question taught that a millennial period, a thousand years, would intervene between Christ's second coming and the destruction of the world by fire. Even Reagan knew he would not live that long. Wallis's critics feel that his efforts to terrorize confused Americans into voting against Reagan on this basis was reprehensible and hardly the action of someone who today deplores "flaming rhetoric and name-calling."[10]

A DIFFERENCE BETWEEN EVANGELICAL AND LIBERAL POLITICAL ACTIVITY

Politically active religious conservatives are doing essentially the same sort of thing that scores of other good American organizations have been doing for decades. Catholic writer Clifford Kossel asks:

Why are the liberal social individualists so worried about [religious conservatives who] push their own interests? They appear to be doing just what other good American organizations do. Corporations, labor unions, senior citizens, NOW [National Organization of Women], NAM [National Association of Manufacturers], and NEA [National Education Association] lobby in federal and state capitals, raise challenges in the courts, use radio, television, and computerized direct mailing to promote their views and get out the voters.[11]

But perhaps there is a difference after all, Kossel observes:

While the other groups seem to be doing mostly the typical American thing in protecting some private interest or reaching for a bigger slice of the federal pie, [religious conservatives take] religion and public morality seriously. Many liberals had thought that, as far as public life was concerned, religion was slowly withering away ... and that "absolutes" were absolutely dead. But here is a religiously based group publicly and militantly proclaiming some absolute positions for insertion into our legal and political ethos.[12]

Political scientist Robert Zwier, hardly a conservative, finds at least one reason to defend the Religious Right:

It is unfair to criticize the new Christian Right for trying to exercise influence over political affairs. To criticize it for violating the wall of separation between church and state is to miss the important distinction between the actions of an institutional church and the convictions of individual Christians. This movement is calling upon persons, not churches, to use their votes to elect certain candidates. That is a fundamental right without which democracy is threatened. Such criticism also ignores the legitimate role which religious beliefs have almost constantly played in establishing this nation and building public policies.[13]

Evangelicals, then, have as much right to attempt to influence public policy as other organizations. After all, this is precisely what theologically and politically liberal Christians have been doing for a long time, and what the evangelical Left has been doing for decades.

ARE EVANGELICALS THE TARGETS OF BIGOTRY?

Many people think evangelicals have been getting unfair treatment from the media, the entertainment industry, and the academic world. Richard John Neuhaus points out: "The pattern in the media and elsewhere is to use the term 'Fundamentalist'[14] in a careless way that refers to anything we deem religiously bizarre or fanatical. . . . This pattern reflects intellectual laziness mixed with an unseemly measure of bigotry."[15]

Another writer who sees some prejudice in recent treatments of conservative Protestants is Nathan Glazer, professor of education at Harvard and an editor of *The Public Interest*, who in the past has collaborated with U.S. Senator Daniel Patrick Moynihan of New York on several studies. Glazer reminds us that religious-based conflicts are not new in American society. Not too long ago, he points out, Catholics were perceived as subversive so far as important American values were concerned.[16]

It is hard to dispute the claim that for decades now, the values of conservative Christians—both Protestant and Roman Catholic—have been under siege in this country. This is apparent in the courts, in the media, in movies and on television, and in the schools. One thing evangelicals want is a reprieve from intolerance against their beliefs, values, and practices.

The Evangelical Reaction Is Defensive

Acording to Glazer, evangelical activity in the public arena should be understood as defensive, not offensive. These actions do not represent a sudden assault on a passive and tolerant society. Rather, they are a reaction to what religious conservatives see as an attack on them and on values that have played an essential role in the success of the American political experiment. As Glazer sees

it, "It is the great successes of secular and liberal forces, princi-
pally operating through the specific agency of the courts, that has
in large measure created the issues on which [evangelicals] have
managed to achieve what influence they have."[17] Glazer provides
several examples to back up his claim.

> Abortion did *not* become an issue because [evangelicals][18]
> wanted to *strengthen* prohibitions against abortion, but
> because liberals wanted to abolish them.... Pornography in
> the 1980s did *not* become an issue because [evangelicals]
> wanted to *ban* D. H. Lawrence, James Joyce, or even Henry
> Miller, but because in the 1960s and 1970s, under-the-table
> pornography moved to the top of the newsstands. Prayer in
> the schools did *not* become an issue because [evangelicals]
> wanted to *introduce* new prayers or sectarian prayers, but
> because the Supreme Court ruled against all prayers. Freedom
> for religious schools became an issue *not* because of any legal
> effort to *expand* their scope, but because the Internal Revenue
> Service and various state authorities tried to impose restric-
> tions on them that private schools had not faced before.[19]

Perhaps the issue of who started these fights is now irrelevant. But it is helpful to remember, as Glazer points out, that

> Dominant power—measured by money, access to the major
> media, influence, the opinion of our educated, moneyed,
> and powerful elites—still rests with the secular and liberal
> forces that created, through court action, the changes that
> have aroused [evangelicalism]. What we are seeing is a
> defensive reaction of the conservative heartland, rather than
> an offensive that intends to or is capable of really upsetting
> the balance, or driving the United States back to the nine-
> teenth century or early twentieth century.[20]

Liberals have been so successful in getting their own agenda
adopted that it is easy for them to forget that "America is a many-cul-
tured society, and that religion is an important component of many
U.S. subcultures as well as of the larger culture."[21] Evangelicals, in

Glazer's opinion, are simply fighting back in an attempt to restore some balance and to regain some lost respect for beliefs and values that are important to them.

Evidence in Support of Glazer's Claim

Ralph Reed of the Christian Coalition has an obvious interest in modern liberalism's discomfort with religion in general and with Christianity in particuar. The hostility of liberals to committed Christians is not a new phenomenon precipitated by their recent reentry into the public arena; it has been part of the liberal creed for decades.

Reed contends that "Extremist groups like People for the American Way attack Christians who run for public office as a threat to the 'separation of church and state,' though they never specify why conservatives are any more of a threat than churchmen and churchwomen on the Left who have led religiously inspired causes for decades."[22]

Reed contends that Democrats have been even more irresponsible in their personal assaults on people of faith who run for public office. He cites the example of how Democrats launched "a vicious campaign of religious bigotry" against Michael Farris, a candidate for lieutenant governor of Virginia. "The incumbent Democratic lieutenant governor," Reed argues, "broadcast television commercials that warned voters that Farris had once worked for Jerry Falwell (he had not) and was supported by Pat Robertson. Newspaper accounts included references to Farris's religion that would have been considered scurrilous if directed at a Jew or a Muslim."[23]

The same thing happened to a Christian businesswoman in Nebraska who announced she would run against U.S. Senator Bob Kerrey. She was attacked as a "Christian Coalition-type" and ridiculed for belonging to an evangelical church.

When Clarence Thomas was nominated to the U.S. Supreme Court in 1991, then-Governor Doug Wilder of Virginia reacted to the news by noting that Thomas "has indicated that he's a very devout Catholic" and asking, "The question is: How much allegiance is there to the Pope?" (Thomas, in fact, is not a Catholic. He attends an Episcopalian church.) These references to a prospective officeholder's religion bear a disturbing resemblance to the paranoid political style of the Know-Nothings of the 1850s. They demonstrate how intolerant some liberals can become when religion creeps beyond the stained-glass ghetto assigned to it.[24]

Congressman Vic Fazio of California, who in 1994 also served as Democratic Congressional Campaign Committee Chair, recently caricatured religious conservatives as "the fire-breathing Christian radical right." In 1993 a *Washington Post* reporter described the religious Right as a group of people who are "largely poor, uneducated, and easy to command."[25] Chapter 4 of Reed's book, *Politically Incorrect*, provides a long list of the intolerant and bigoted acts evangelicals have encountered. In several of the more egregious instances, he reports:

The *New York Times* published an editorial on its opinion page in 1993 that asserted that the religious conservative movement "confronts us with a far greater threat than the old threat of Communism." Earlier, the *Times* printed a column by Garry Wills that said of evangelicals in the Republican Party: "The crazies are in charge. The fringe has taken over." A syndicated columnist has suggested that "we tax the hell out of the churches if they open their holy yaps one more time about abortion, prayer in the schools or anything else." Some of this is mere hyperbole. . . . Still, the impression conveyed by these statements suggests that religion is irrational, intolerant, and possibly dangerous.[26]

One must wonder how long we must wait until signers of *The Cry for Renewal* condemn *these* outrageous examples of "fire-breathing rhetoric and name-calling." Noting the irony of the situation, Reed deplores how "The crooked finger of suspicion once pointed at [John F. Kennedy during his 1960 campaign] is indeed directed today at Baptists, fundamentalists, and pro-life Roman Catholics."[27]

ANSWERS TO CRITICS OF THE CHRISTIAN COALITION

Reed wants people to understand that the Christian Coalition is neither a church, a denomination, nor a ministry. It is a voluntary organization composed of individual citizens who happen to be believers who wish to share their faith and witness to others.[28] When asked to respond to people who are afraid of the Coalition, Reed says:

> we are probably no different than any social movement that is moving from marginalization to full integration into the public life of our nation. I think the first thing we have to do is to overcome the stereotype which in the infamous phrase of the *Washington Post* is "poor, uneducated, and easy to command." The notion that these are a lot of ... ignorant fundamentalist hicks coming out of the bog ... [is] a stereotype which is deep and abiding in the 20th century.[29]

In point of fact, 12 percent of Christian Coalition members hold a Ph.D. or other advanced degree as in law or medicine. The national average for these levels of academic achievement is 10 percent.[30]

Reed insists that the Christian Coalition's agenda is mainstream.[31] He condemns violence at abortion clinics.[32] He disputes claims that the Coalition wants to turn America into a "Victorian, patriarchal, proto-Nazi, crypto-Klansman, theocratic police state."[33] If Reed had his way, America would be a society in which "Jews, women, racial minorities, and those of differing faith traditions would be free from discrimination and bias."[34] He rejects charges

> that if religious conservatives held office they would destroy public education, outlaw contraception, ban the teaching of evolution, destroy the First Amendment, censor books, and force women out of the workplace and back into the kitchen. These accusations are grounded not in fact but in fear and bigotry. This book [Reed's *Politically Incorrect*]

addresses how that stereotype has been broadcast by our secular culture and, tragically, reinforced by some of us with deep faith.[35]

When asked what religious conservatives really want, Reed answers;

They want a place at the table in the conversation we call democracy [Does the religious Left intend to deny them this opportunity?] Their commitment to pluralism includes a place for faith among the many other competing interests in society. For too long, we have left politics to the special interests. It is time for the values of middle America to have their place at the table. For decades religious people have been on the sidelines watching everyone else play the game. They want to be on the field, if not always to win, then at least to participate. If they should win, they do not want to have victory denied them because of their religious beliefs.[36]

Reed answers still another objection raised by the Religious Left:

In seeking to redress their cultural isolation, people of faith must resist the temptation to promote political involvement as the sole answer to our social ills. The church that saves souls and restores marriages gains a platform from which it can speak to the broader society. The hand that feeds, clothes, and educates is strong enough to bang the gavel in the courthouse and state house. A caring faith community will not merely condemn the abortionist, but offer loving alternatives for women, such as homes for unwed mothers and adoption services.[37]

Reed complains that the media and other Coalition critics ignore their compassion and charitable efforts. They also misrepresent Coalition thinking about government welfare:

I don't think we should completely dismantle it [the welfare system], and I don't think the Christian Coalition has ever taken the position that the government has no role in helping to take care of the most needy among us. Our objection is not to the idea of a limited role of government in the work of charity. It is the idea of a bloated, corrupt, counterproductive, failed, modern liberal welfare state. We're trying to reform a welfare state that has had the opposite of its intended effect upon everyone.[38]

Reed acknowledges that religious conservatives have made their share of mistakes—which only proves their humanity. But as this book has shown, conservatives do not have a monopoly on saying and doing stupid things.

In a recent issue of *Christianity Today,* William F. Buckley Jr. was asked to assess the growing influence of religious conservatives in America. He offered the opinion that "What we see here is a mobilization of people who are properly horrified by what they see going on in Hollywood, in the growth of single-parent families, and so forth. They've figured out that our foundations need restoring, and I have never doubted that those foundations are religious."[39]

But Buckley also had a warning for leaders of the Christian Coalition and other groups that speak out on social issues. "What frightens people most about the Religious Right," he said, "is the rhetoric that is sometimes used." Michael Cromartie, Buckley's interviewer, picked up his point and added, "The Christian Right, then, would do well to learn how to use rhetoric in a way that is Christian and appeals to a public that doesn't believe in Christian theology?" Buckley's reply obviously was affirmative.

Ralph Reed has shown his own appreciation for this criticism. Whether a more responsible use of rhetoric in the future will help alleviate the misunderstanding and concern many people have with regard to Christian conservatives is something that bears watching. At the same time, it would be nice to think that more people in the media would get their facts straight and at least appear less prejudicial to people of faith who have no plans to take over the country.

Notes

Chapter One: Is There a Religious Left?

1. See Marvin Olasky, *Prodigal Press* (Westchester, IL: Crossway Books, 1988). Olasky is a professor of journalism at the University of Texas, Austin, and the editor of *World*, an evangelical magazine.

2. It is proper to point out that many signers of *The Cry for Renewal* are not an essential part of the Religious Left. People sign documents for all kinds of reasons, not all of them having to do with a grasp of the issues or the full agenda of the people behind the document. Signers of the document who are discussed in this book are members of the Religious Left; there are a number of other signers who may not be.

3. Rich Lowry, "Clinton's Revelation," *National Review* (March 7, 1994), 52.

4. See Ronald Nash, *Poverty and Wealth: Why Socialism Doesn't Work* (Dallas: Probe Books, 1992), chap. 16.

5. Michael Cromartie, "Fixing the World," *Christianity Today* (April 27, 1992), 25.

6. Ibid.

Chapter Two: Political Liberalism in American Mainline and Catholic Churches

1. Many of my books provide support for this claim and illustrate the nature of these deviant theologies. As examples, see *Is Jesus the Only Savior?* (Grand Rapids: Zondervan, 1994); *The Word of God and the Mind of Man* (Phillipsburg, NJ: Presbyterian and Reformed, 1992); *Evangelicals in America* (Nashville: Abingdon, 1987); *Evangelical Renewal in the Mainline Churches* (Westchester, IL: Crossway, 1987); *Process Theology* (Grand Rapids: Baker, 1987); and *Beyond Liberation Theology* (Grand Rapids: Baker, 1992).

2. Emilio Nuñez, *Liberation Theology* (Chicago: Moody Press, 1985), 37.

3. Friedrich Hayek, *Law, Legislation and Liberty*, vol. 2 (Chicago: University of Chicago Press, 1976), 66.

4. See K. L. Billingsley, *The Generation That Knew Not Josef* (Portland, OR: Multnomah Press, 1985). The "Josef" in the play on words in Billingsley's title was Josef Stalin, not the Hebrew Joseph whose deeds saved Egypt from starvation (see Exodus 1:8).

5. Paul Seabury, "Trendier Than Thou," *Harper's* (October 1978), 40.

6. Rael Jean Isaac and Erich Isaac, *The Coercive Utopians* (Chicago: Regnery Gateway, 1983), 2.

7. Ibid.

8. Ibid., 3.

9. Ibid., 4.

10. Ibid., 18.

11. See ibid., 19.

12. See ibid., 20.

13. Ibid., 26.

14. See ibid., 29.

15. (New York: Oxford University Press, 1992).

16. Cited in *Destructive Generation* by Peter Collier and David Horowitz (New York: Summit Books, 1989), 151.

17. Hollander, *Anti-Americanism*, 127.

18. Ibid., 128.

19. Ibid., 143.

20. See Hollander, *Anti-Americanism*, 122.

21. K. L. Billingsley, *From Mainline to Sideline: The Social Witness of the National Council of Churches* (Washington, DC: Ethics and Public Policy Center, 1990), 188.

22. Ibid., 189.

23. See Richard John Neuhaus, *The Catholic Moment* (San Francisco: Harper & Row, 1987).

24. See Paul Gottfried, *The Conservative Movement*, rev. ed. (New York: Twayne, 1993), 36.

25. Ibid., 35.

26. For more on this document, see Ronald Nash, *Poverty and Wealth: Why Socialism Doesn't Work* (Richardson, TX: Probe Books, 1992), 2–3.

27. See Hollander, *Anti-Americanism*, 100.

28. Consistent with the liberal dogma that there are no real liberals, only moderates, supporters of liberation theology deny this. Their denial is easily refuted, as Humberto Belli and I have done in our book *Beyond Liberation Theology* (Grand Rapids: Baker, 1992). Belli was a Marxist in his native Nicaragua during the 1970s, but he abandoned that system after converting to Christianity. During the years of Sandinista rule in Nicaragua, Belli lived in exile in the United States. Following Nicaragua's recovery of democracy in 1989, Belli returned to Managua, where he has served as minister of education in the government of Violeta Barrios de Chamorro.

29. The real issue in the dispute between theologically liberal Roman Catholics and Pope John Paul II is theological unbelief. Richard John Neuhaus is correct when he states that the Pope "is exercised *not about dissent but about apostasy*. He is attempting to chart a Christian course that is not so much against modernity as it is beyond modernity. The only modernity to be discarded is the *debased modernity of unbelief* that results in a prideful and premature closure of the world against its promised destiny" (Neuhaus, *The Catholic Moment*, 284).

30. Neuhaus, *The Catholic Moment*, 172–73.

31. Theological pluralism denies that Jesus Christ is the only Savior of the world. For a detailed account and critique of pluralism, see Ronald Nash, *Is Jesus The Only Savior?* (Grand Rapids: Zondervan, 1994).

32. Neuhaus, *The Catholic Moment*, 172–73.

33. See Hollander, *Anti-Americanism*, 114.

34. For more on this, see Nash and Belli, *Beyond Liberation Theology*.

35. Hollander, *Anti-Americanism*, 114.

36. Isaac and Isaac, *The Coercive Utopians*, 33.

37. Ibid., 35.

38. Billingsley, *The Generation That Knew Not Josef*, 204.

39. Ibid.

40. Ibid., 205.

41. Ibid.

42. Ibid., 207.

43. Theological liberals have typically rejected such orthodox Christian beliefs as the Trinity, the deity of Christ, the Incarnation, the Atonement, and the Resurrection; they also are lukewarm in their appreciation for Scripture as the inspired Word of God. While the evangelical liberals in view in this book are often divided over the matter of biblical inerrancy, some of them see the Bible as an inscripturation of God's special revelation to humankind. Others also manifest the growing tendency within evangelical circles to drift toward a neo-liberal or neo-orthodox view of Scripture. For an account of this, see my books *The Word of God and the Mind of Man* (Phillipsburg, NJ: Presbyterian and Reformed, 1992), and *The Closing of the American Heart* (Richardson, TX: Probe Books, 1990), chap. 11.

44. In my judgment, this qualification is made necessary by doubts about a few people in the evangelical Left whom some think have wandered away from a more solid evangelical commitment that seemed evident in their younger days.

Chapter Three: The Adversary Generation

1. Several of my books discuss this in greater detail. See *Freedom, Justice and the State* (Lanham, MD: University Press of America, 1980); *Social Justice and the Christian Church* (Lanham, MD: University Press of America, 1990); and *Poverty and Wealth* (Dallas: Probe Books, 1992).

2. I appreciate the help of Dr. Ron Taber in putting this material together.

3. This point must be noted carefully. When Jim Wallis criticizes liberal Democrats in the mid-1990s, it is important to ask whether he is doing this from the perspective of his New Left ideology.

4. Once again, it is important to ask whether Jim Wallis's recent call for decentralized decision making in the mid-1990s is simply another expression of earlier New Left thinking.

5. Peter Collier and David Horowitz, *Destructive Generation* (New York: Summit Books, 1989), 145.

6. Ibid., 148.

7. See Paul Hollander, *The Survival of the Adversary Culture* (New Brunswick, NJ: Transaction Books, 1988).

8. Ibid., 14.

9. Georgie Anne Geyer, "Marxists on Campus" (August 29, 1989).

10. Ibid.

11. Nicaraguan Humberto Belli tells the story of these events in *Breaking Faith: The Sandinista Revolution and Its Impact on Freedom and Faith in Nicaragua* (Westchester, IL: Crossway Books, 1985).

12. K. L. Billingsley, *From Mainline to Sideline: The Social Witness of the National Council of Churches* (Washington, DC: Ethics and Public Policy Center, 1990), 110.

13. See Belli, *Breaking Faith*, 72.

14. Cited by Billingsley, *From Mainline to Sideline*, 111.

15. See Billingsley, *From Mainline to Sideline*, 110.

16. See Collier and Horowitz, *Destructive Generation*, 154ff.

17. Ibid., 157ff.

18. Cited in Edward Cain, "Nicaraguan Christians Supported the Revolution," *Signposts* 5, no. 4 (1986): 2.

19. Cited in "D'Escoto Comes Clean," *Crisis* (January 1988), 2.

20. For an interesting look at a dispute among several Calvin College professors over such trips and related manifestations of political radicalism, see the editorial by Professor Edward E. Ericson, Jr., in the August 1985 issue of the *Reformed Journal*. It is worth noting that Ericson is the author of a book about the Soviet dissident Aleksandr Solzhenitsyn.

21. Tom Carson, "The Long Way Back," *Village Voice* (May 12, 1987), 7.

22. Paul Hollander, *Anti-Americanism* (New York: Oxford University Press, 1992), 264. See Hollander's detailed bibliography, 487–90.

23. Martin Peretz, "Cambridge Diarist—Out of Line," *New Republic* (April 7, 1986).

24. Paul Berman, "Nicaragua 1986-Notes on the Sandinista Revolution," *Mother Jones* (December 20, 1986), 20, 22.

25. See José Míguez Bonino, *Christians and Marxists* (Grand Rapids: Eerdmans, 1976), 25–26.

26. For more on this, see Humberto Belli, "Nicaragua: Field Test for Liberation Theology," *Pastoral Renewal* (September 1984): 30–31.

27. For more specifics about all this, see Belli, *Breaking Faith*.

28. Again, see Belli's *Breaking Faith* for more details.

29. See *Time* (June 24, 1991), 34.

30. Tom Sine, *Cease Fire: Searching for Sanity in America's Culture War* (Grand Rapids: Eerdmans, 1995), 44.

31. Billingsley, *From Mainline to Sideline*, 143.

Chapter Four: Of Marx and Men

1. Paul Hollander, *Political Pilgrims* (New York: Oxford University Press, 1981), 416–17.

2. Ibid., 417. See also Paul Hollander, *The Many Faces of Socialism* (New Brunswick, NJ: Transaction Books, 1983), 8, 9.

3. José Míguez Bonino, *Christians and Marxists* (Grand Rapids: Eerdmans, 1976), 115.

4. Ibid., 76.

5. Ibid., 77.

6. Peter Berger, "Underdevelopment Revisited," *Commentary* (July 1984), 43.

7. Míguez Bonino, *Christians and Marxists*, 90.

8. Andrew Kirk, *The Good News of the Kingdom Coming* (Downers Grove, IL: InterVarsity Press, 1985), 73.

9. Ibid., 44, 45.

10. There is a fourth variety of Marxism that I do not have space to discuss in this book. It is sometimes called "chameleon Marxism" because of the ease with which its pro-

ponents adapt to different situations. See Ronald Nash, *The Closing of the American Heart* (Dallas: Probe Books, 1990), chap. 8.

11. An example would be Norman Thomas, who was for years the best-known advocate of democratic socialism in the United States.

12. For discussions of these objections, see two of my books, *Social Justice and the Christian Church* (Lanham, MD: University Press of America, 1992) and *Freedom, Justice and the State* (Lanham, MD: University Press of America, 1980).

13. See Anthony Campolo, *We Have Met the Enemy, and They Are Partly Right* (Waco, TX: Word, 1985), chaps. 7–9.

14. For one example, see Tony Campolo, *Carpe Diem: Seize the Day* (Dallas: Word, 1994), chap. 6. The entire chapter is vintage Marcuse. On pages 144–45 of the book Campolo delivers undeserved praise for some of Marcuse's ideas. For information about how the Marcusian theories that Campolo finds so enthralling lead to totalitarianism, see my book *Freedom, Justice and the State*, 140–45.

15. Campolo is clearly familiar with Marcuse's ideas. My point is that Campolo and other Christian sociologists seem unaware of the extent to which Marcuse manipulated Marx's ambiguous early writings to suit his own purposes.

16. I document the totalitarian nature of Marcuse's political theories in my book *Freedom, Justice and the State*, chap. 3.

17. For an important argument showing that Marx actually repudiated the notion of alienation, see Daniel Bell, *The End of Ideology* (New York: Free Press, 1960), 344. See also Daniel Bell, "The 'Rediscovery' of Alienation," *Journal of Philosophy* 56 (1959): 933–52. Even in the *Communist Manifesto*, Sidney Hook argues, "Marx explicitly disavows the theory of alienation as 'metaphysical rubbish,' as a linguistic German mystification of social phenomena described by French social critics" (Sidney Hook, *Marxism and Beyond* [Totawa, NJ: Rowman & Littlefield, 1983], 48).

Chapter Five: Jim Wallis and the Sojourners Movement

1. The others, as far as this book is concerned, are Tony Campolo and Ron Sider.

2. K. L. Billingsley, "PC Agit-Prophet," *Heterodoxy* (January 1995), 1. Billingsley's perceptive article is one of the few extended analyses of Wallis and his work. Billingsley is also intrigued by the clever way that Wallis seeks to reinvent or repackage himself.

3. Jim Wallis, "Liberating and Conformity," *Sojourners* (September 1976), 3–4.

4. Quoted by Billingsley, "PC Agit-Propohet," 1.

5. *National Review* (September 11, 1995), 11.

6. Ibid.

7. Ibid.

8. See Billingsley, "PC Agit-Prophet," 9.

9. Jim Wallis, "Back to Normal, Arrogantly," *Sojourners* (November 1976), 4.

10. Jim Wallis, "Compassion Not Politics for Refugees," *Sojourners* (September 1975).

11. Paul Hollander, *Anti-Americanism* (New York: Oxford University Press, 1992), 140.

12. K. L. Billingsley, *The Generation That Knew Not Josef* (Portland, OR: Multnomah Press, 1985), 175–76.

13. See Billingsley, "PC-Agit Prophet," 9.

14. Ibid.

15. Rael Jean Isaac and Erich Isaach, *The Coercive Utopians* (Chicago: Regnery Gateway, 1983), 7.

16. Hollander, *Anti-Americanism,* 144.

17. Billingsley, "PC Agit-Prophet," 9.

18. Hollander, *Anti-Americanism,* 144–45.

19. Billingsley, "PC Agit-Prophet," 9. Billingsley's source was a former official at the foundation where Wallis sought his grant in the late 1980s.

20. Billingsley, "PC-Agit Prophet," 9.

21. Ibid.

22. See ibid., 9.

23. Ibid.

24. Jim Wallis, "Marginal Notes," *Sojourners* (December 1982), 27.

25. Ibid.

26. (San Francisco: Harper & Row, 1984), 56–72.

27. Dean C. Curry and Myron S. Augsburger, "The Perils of Contemporary Pacifism," *Nuclear Arms: Two Views on World Peace* (Waco, TX: Word Books, 1987), 121.

28. Hollander, *Anti-Americanism,* 101.

29. "A Matter of Idolatry," *Sojourners* (March 1984).

30. Ibid.

31. Jim Wallis, "Marginal Notes," *Sojourners* (October 1983), 13.

32. Billingsley, *The Generation That Knew Not Josef,* 150.

33. Billingsley, "PC-Agit Prophet," 9.

34. See ibid., 10.

35. See "Nicaragua: A Fragile Future," *Sojourners* (March 1983).

36. Billingsley, "PC-Agit Prophet," 10.

37. The book is *The Rise of Christian Conscience,* ed. Jim Wallis (San Francisco: Harper & Row, 1987).

38. Hollander, *Anti-Americanism,* 102.

39. Michael Cromartie of the Ethics and Public Policy Center states that evangelical Left magazines "are now more influential among left-wing Catholics and liberal Protestants (with the latter's membership declining rapidly). Once thought to be the wave of future evangelical social thought, the radical magazine's popular support has diminished significantly" ("Fixing the World," *Christianity Today* [April 27, 1992], 25).

40. P. xxviii.

41. Jim Wallis, *The Soul of Politics* (Maryknoll, NY: Orbis Books, 1994), 36. Nothing in this paragraph should be taken to mean that I equate evangelicalism, fundamentalism, and the Religious Right.

42. Ibid., 108.

Chapter Six: Up Against the Wallis

1. Clark Pinnock, "A Pilgrimage in Political Theology," *Liberation Theology,* ed. Ronald Nash (Grand Rapids: Baker, 1988), 106.

2. Ibid., 111.

3. Ibid.

4. Ibid., 112.

5. Ibid.

6. Ibid., 114.

7. *The Road to Damascus: Kairos and Conversion*, published jointly by the Catholic Institute for International Relations (London), the Center of Concern (Washington, DC), and Christian Aid (London), 1989, 1.

8. Ibid.

9. George Weigel, "Still Blind, On the Road to Damascus," *American Purpose* (November 1989), 65.

10. Richard John Neuhaus, "Ambushed on the Road to Damascus," *First Things* (April 1990): 66.

11. Weigel, "Still Blind, On the Road to Damascus," 66–67.

12. Tony Campolo, *Is Jesus a Republican or a Democrat?* (Dallas: Word Books, 1995), and Tom Sine, *Cease Fire: Searching for Sanity in America's Culture Wars* (Grand Rapids: Eerdmans, 1995).

13. Jim Wallis, *The Soul of Politics* (Maryknoll, NY: Orbis Books, 1994).

14. Ibid., 7.

15. Ibid., 20.

16. Ibid.

17. Ibid., 20–21.

18. Ibid., 22.

19. Ibid.

20. Ibid., 26–27.

21. See ibid., 109–11.

22. Wallis's discussion of homosexuality appears on pages 111–13 of *The Soul of Politics*.

23. The actions in question include public nudity and simulated sex acts.

24. Joel Shuman, "Where Lies Our Hope?" *Prism* 2, no. 1 (November–December 1994): 24–25.

25. Ibid., 24.

26. Ibid.

27. Ibid., 25.

28. In spite of the 1993 date, the essay appeared while Wallis's book was in press.

29. Jim Wallis, "As If Values Mattered," *Sojourners* (November–December 1993), 4. For a book-length argument defending the necessary role of a market system in preserving the enviroment, see Joseph L. Bast, Peter J. Hill, and Richard C. Ruse, *Eco-Sanity: A Common Sense Guide to Environmentalism* (Lanham, MD: James Madison Books, 1994).

30. Ibid.

31. Ibid.

32. Jim Wallis, "To the Highest Bidder," *Sojourners* (November-December 1995), 18.

33. For my own statement of this kind of approach, see Ronald Nash, *Freedom, Justice and the State* (Lanham, MD: University Press of America, 1980), and Ronald Nash, *Social Justice and the Christian Church* (Milford, MI: Mott Media, 1983). The second book was later published by Baker Book House and University Press of America.

34. Wallis, "To the Highest Bidder," 19.

35. Ibid., 19.

36. Ibid., 20.

37. Richard John Neuhaus, "Repression Envy and 'Biblical Politics,'" *Religion and Society Report* (March 1988), 6.

38. Quoted by K. L. Billingsley, "PC-Agit Prophet," *Heterodoxy* (January 1995), 10.

39. Ibid.

40. Ibid.

Chapter Seven: Rich Christians and Ron Sider

1. Ralph Reed, *Politically Incorrect* (Dallas: Word, 1994), 215–16.

2. For the text of the document, see Ronald J. Sider, ed., *The Chicago Declaration* (Carol Stream, IL: Creation House, 1974).

3. (Grand Rapids: Eerdmans, 1947).

4. Carl Henry made these comments in personal correspondence with this writer, postmarked December 1, 1995. Used by permission.

5. Sider's current publication is called *Prism*.

6. (Downers Grove, IL: InterVarsity Press, 1987).

7. For a fair description of this movement, see Ronald Nash, *Great Divides* (Colorado Springs: NavPress, 1993), chap. 2.

8. Sider's recognition of some of these errors led to a major rewriting of the book for its second edition, with assistance from some people trained in economics.

9. George Mavrodes, "On Helping the Hungry," *Christianity Today* (December 30, 1977), 46. Mavrodes's essay also contains interesting observations about Sider's call for Christians to reduce their standard of living.

10. Robert Frykenberg, "World Hunger: Food Is Not the Answer," *Christianity Today* (December 11, 1981), 36.

11. See Ronald J. Sider, "Rich Christians in an Age of Hunger—Revisited," *Discernment* (Spring 1995), 2–3, 6–7. The essay was originally an address given at Wheaton College in 1995.

12. For example, Stephen Charles Mott, who was at that time a professor at Gordon-Conwell Theological Seminary, saw the Jubilee Year as a divine endorsement of this kind of thinking. See Mott's *Biblical Ethics and Social Change* (New York: Oxford University Press, 1982), chap. 4.

13. At one time this was Sider's euphemism for capitalism.

14. Sider, *Rich Christians in an Age of Hunger*, 1st ed. (1977), 88.

15. See p. 75.

16. Sider repeated these claims during a joint public appearance he and I made at Houghton College in October 1988.

17. E. Calvin Beisner, *Prosperity and Poverty* (Westchester, IL: Crossway Books, 1988), 64. For a statement of my criticism of Sider written in 1982, see Ronald Nash, *Social Justice and the Christian Church* (Milford, MI: Mott Media, 1983), chap. 6.

18. As a matter of fact, the Jubilee principle was never instituted.

19. Or, to be correct, *renter*.

20. Properly, *renter*.

21. Ibid., 3.

22. He specifically cites page 114 of the first edition in this connection.

23. "Rich Christians in an Age of Hunger—Revisited," 6.

24. Ibid.

25. Ibid.

26. Ibid.

27. Ibid.

28. The persistent Whitewater Land Development problems of President and Mrs. Clinton have been described as examples of such behavior. See James R. Stewart, *Blood Sport* (New York: Simon & Schuster, 1996).

29. For the Old Testament view on this subject, see Ecclesiastes 5:19: "Moreover, when God gives any man wealth and possessions, and enables him to enjoy them, to accept his lot and be happy in his work—this is a gift of God."

30. See Luke 16:1–3; 19:11–27; Matt. 25:24–30. These parables also commend those who demonstrate their ability to increase their wealth.

31. (Downers Grove, IL: InterVarsity Press, 1982).

32. Keith B. Payne and Karl I. Payne, *A Just Defense* (Portland, OR: Multnomah Press, 1987), 120. For examples of this tactic in the Sider-Taylor book, see pages 213, 273–92.

33. K. L. Billingsley, *The Generation That Knew Not Josef* (Portland, OR: Multnomah Press, 1987), 188.

34. Payne and Payne, *A Just Defense,* 55.

35. Ibid. The Paynes' book is a helpful examination of several questions related to the issue of whether limited use of strategic nuclear weapons can satisfy the conditions of traditional Just War theory. Their argument strikes at the very heart of Sider's case for nuclear pacifism.

36. Tim Stafford, "Ron Sider's Unsettling Crusade," *Christianity Today* (April 27, 1992), 18.

37. Ibid., 19.

Chapter Eight: Sider on Peace, Justice, and Life

1. Evangelical opponents of abortion do disagree sometimes about what should be done in cases of pregnancies resulting from rape or incest.

2. For evidence supporting this, see Ronald Nash, *Great Divides* (Colorado Springs: NavPress, 1993), chap. 1. For a defense of abortion by a former Southern Baptist seminary professor, see Paul D. Simmons, *A Theological Response to Fundamentalism on the Abortion Issue* (Washington, DC: Religious Coalition for Abortion Rights Educational Fund, 1985). For a defense of abortion by a radical Christian feminist, see Virginia Mollenkott, "Reproductive Choice: Basic to Justice for Women," *Christian Scholars Review* 17 (1987–1988): 286–93.

3. See Ronald J. Sider, *Completely Pro-Life* (Downers Grove, IL: InterVarsity, 1987).

4. Ibid., 44.

5. Ibid.

6. Ronald J. Sider, "Abortion Is Not the Only Issue," *Christianity Today* (July 14, 1989), 28.

7. Richard John Neuhaus, *Religion and Society Report* (October 1988), 3.

8. Ibid., 5.

9. Ibid., 4.

10. For my own thinking about Third World poverty, see Ronald Nash, *Poverty and Wealth* (Dallas: Probe Books, 1992), chap. 17.

11. Neuhaus, *Religion and Society Report,* 5.

12. Ibid., 4.

13. Ibid.

14. Charles E. White, "Why Abortion Matters Most," *Christianity Today* (July 14, 1989), 35.

15. Ibid.

16. Ibid., 34.

17. Ibid., 36.

18. While a social liberal, Hatfield is strongly pro-life. But Sider's 1988 scorecard made Hatfield look weaker than more radical liberals such as Metzenbaum, Cranston, and Kennedy.

19. For more detail, see Nash, *Poverty and Wealth,* 121–24.

20. Neuhaus, *Religion and Society Report,* 4.

21. White, "Why Abortion Matters Most," 36.

22. Ibid.

23. Dean C. Curry, *World Without Tyranny* (Westchester, IL: Crossway Books, 1989), 103.

24. Ibid., 104.

25. Evidence reveals that less than 25 percent of tax dollars collected to help the poor ever reaches the poor.

26. M. Stanton Evans, *Clear and Present Dangers* (New York: Harcourt Brace Jovanovich, 1975), 127.

27. Brian Griffiths, *The Creation of Wealth* (Downers Grove, IL: InterVarsity Press, 1985), 60.

Chapter Nine: Tony Campolo and *Is Jesus a Republican or a Democrat?*

1. Tom Sine, *Cease Fire: Searching for Sanity in America's Culture Wars* (Grand Rapids: Eerdmans, 1995).

2. Tony Campolo, *Is Jesus a Republican or a Democrat?* (Dallas: Word Books, 1995).

3. An untitled and anonymous review of Sine's *Cease Fire* in *First Things* (November 1995), 70.

4. Campolo, *Is Jesus a Republican or a Democrat?*, xvi.

5. Ibid.

6. Ibid., xviii.

7. Ibid., 1–2.

8. Ibid.

9. Ibid., 3–4.

10. Ibid., 4. For the record, the U.S. economy is not a laissez faire system.

11. See *Time* (August 14, 1989).

12. For more on this, see Ronald Nash, *The Closing of the American Heart: What's Really Wrong With America's Schools* (Dallas: Probe Books, 1990).

13. Campolo, *Is Jesus a Republican or a Democrat?*, 4.

14. Ibid.

15. Ibid., 4–5.

16. Ibid., 7.

17. Ibid., 13.

18. Ibid.

19. Ibid.

20. Ibid.

21. It is difficult to know exactly what is intended in Campolo's imprecise language in this sentence. One trusts he is not calling for unstructured action, something the radical SDS would have welcomed back in the sixties. It is important to stress that local efforts at the neighborhood level will be tied to mediating institutions such as churches that have an organizational structure responsible for making decisions, developing budgets, raising funds, and sharing accountability.

22. Campolo, *Is Jesus a Republican or a Democrat?*, 13.

23. Ibid., 14.

24. Ibid., 15.

25. Ibid.

26. Ibid., 160–61.

27. Ibid., 161.

28. Ibid., 162.

29. Ibid., 163.

30. See the Crossway Books edition of my *Poverty and Wealth* (published in 1988), 181–82.

31. See Peter Berger and Richard John Neuhaus, *To Empower People: The Role of Mediating Institutions in Public Policy* (Washington, DC: American Enterprise Institute, 1977).

32. Unpublished comments from the Center on Religion and Society Conference, quoted in Nash, *Poverty and Wealth*, 182.

33. For more on all this, including positive suggestions not considered by Campolo, see Nash, *Poverty and Wealth*, chap. 17.

34. Campolo, *Is Jesus a Republican or a Democrat?*, 145.

Chapter Ten: Campolo's Responses to Four Questions

1. Responsible writers on the question agree on the importance of distinguishing between homosexual inclinations and overt homosexual conduct.

2. Stanton L. Jones, "The Loving Opposition," *Christianity Today* (July 19, 1993), 20.

3. Ibid. Italics in the original.

4. Campolo also argues for the ordination of homosexuals, but neglects to clarify whether this applies to all homosexuals or only to people with homosexual inclinations who are living celibate lives.

5. See preface by Tony Campolo in his book *Is Jesus a Republican or a Democrat?* (Dallas: Word Books, 1995).

6. See Tony Campolo, *20 Hot Potatoes Christians Are Afraid to Touch* (Dallas: Word, 1988), 111–12.

7. Ibid., 115.

8. Ibid.

9. Tony Campolo, "What About Homophobia?" *Prism* (February 1994), 20.

10. Ibid.

11. Ibid.

12. See Midge Decter, "Dying of the Light," *National Review* (November 27, 1995), 36–40. Decter, citing the 187,309 new cases of AIDS reported for the years 1993 and 1994, asks, "Is it, then, willful suicide, or hubris ... that has lately been leading so many young homosexuals knowingly to engage in the kind of unprotected sex that is most calculated to leave them with AIDS?" (36).

13. Austin Pryor, "Editorial," *SMI* 6, no. 9 (1995): 2. *SMI* stands for Sound Mind Investing.

14. Jones, "The Loving Opposition," 25.

15. Ibid.

16. Christina Hoff Sommers, "Feminism and the College Curriculum," *Imprimis* (June 1990), 2.

17. Ibid., 4.

18. See Campolo, *Is Jesus a Republican or a Democrat?*, chap. 6. In spite of this rejection of gender-feminism, many evangelicals will find the chapter disappointing for other reasons.

19. My own account of the biblical and theological dimensions of the debate can be found in my book *Great Divides* (Colorado Springs: NavPress, 1993), chaps. 2–3.

20. See Tony Campolo, *How to Rescue the Earth Without Worshipping Nature* (Nashville: Thomas Nelson, 1992) and Ronald J. Sider, "Redeeming the Environmentalists," *Christianity Today* (June 21, 1993), 26–29.

21. Wilbur L. Bullock, in a book review in *Perspectives on Science and Christian Faith* 45 (1993): 138.

22. Campolo, *How to Rescue the Earth*, 71.

23. Ibid., 38.

24. Ibid., 40.

25. Bullock, book review, 138.

26. Of course, there is intense debate whether global warning is occurring and what its causes might be.

27. Michael S. Coffman, *Saviors of the Earth?* (Chicago: Northfield, 1994).

28. This is one of Ron Sider's points in his article "Redeeming the Environmentalists."

29. Albert Gore, *Earth in the Balance: Ecology and the Human Spirit* (Boston: Houghton Mifflin, 1992).

30. (Lanham, MD: Madison Books, 1994). Peter J. Hill is a professor of economics at Wheaton College.

31. Ibid., 243.

32. Ibid., 226.

33. Ibid.

34. Ibid., 227.

35. Tony Campolo, *Can Mainline Denominations Make a Comeback?* (Valley Forge, PA: Judson Press, 1995).

36. See *Evangelical Renewal in the Mainline Churches,* ed. Ronald Nash (Westchester, IL: Crossway Books, 1987).

37. Robert W. Patterson, in a review of *Can Mainline Denominations Make a Comeback?* in *Christianity Today* (October 23, 1995), 71.

38. Ibid.

39. I understand fully that there are few words I could use that would raise the ire of evangelical liberals more quickly than "anti-American." Perhaps I use it here simply to test the maturity of their newfound centrist sentiments. The evangelical Left has maintained that every Christian's first allegiance is to God and his kingdom. No evangelical conservative disputes this. But then the evangelical Left has gone further and maintained that we owe no special allegiance to the United States. This, we dispute. The role of the Christian faith in the early centuries of this nation is a complex matter. So, too, is the purity of the American vision over the centuries. But conservative Christians do not believe that love of country is a sin.

Chapter Eleven: The Silence of the Lambs: President Clinton and the Evangelical Left

1. Representatives of the Left have attacked every president from Johnson to Bush. Reagan especially received unconscionable treatment at their hands.

2. Cited by Rich Lowry, "Clinton's Revelation," *National Review* (March 7, 1994), 52.

3. See James R. Stewart, *Blood Sport* (New York: Simon & Schuster, 1996), 69–71, 170–74, 319–24, 348–52, 357–58, 386–90, 421–22.

4. On January 9, 1996, a federal appeals court panel in St. Louis ruled against the President's legal attempt to get the suit postponed until after he leaves office. The President's attorney has promised further appeals, even to the Supreme Court if necessary. For one evangelical publication's account of all this, see Roy Maynard, "Who's Marching for Paula Jones?" in *World* (April 30, 1994), 10–13. Maynard's title refers to the fact that feminists who typically pursue any allegation of sexual harassment refused to come to the assistance of Paula Jones.

5. Ralph Reed, head of the Christian Coalition, rejects liberal claims that his organization was involved in raising funds to help Paula Jones's legal expenses. The *Washington Post* later retracted the charge. See Ralph Reed, *Politically Incorrect* (Dallas: Word Books, 1994), 68.

6. James R. Stewart discusses the draft issue on page 198 of *Blood Sport.*

7. The most thorough account of the Whitewater affair thus far appears in Stewart's *Blood Sport.*

8. John H. Fund, "Is the Net Closing In? Part 1," *National Review* (December 1995), 16.

9. Ibid.

10. Cited by Fund, "Is the Net Closing In?" 16. Given his impeccable liberal credentials, no one can accuse Matthews of being part of the Religious Right.

11. Senator D'Amato is chairman of the Senate Committee investigating Whitewater and White House events that followed the death of Vincent Foster.

12. Fund, "Is The Net Closing In? Part I," 17.

13. Ibid.

14. Liberal concurrence with many or all of the allegations I have mentioned has been evident on all of the following television programs, among others: *The McLaughlin Group, The Capitol Gang, Inside Politics, Meet the Press, The David Brinkley Show,* and *Inside Washington*.

15. The resignation was prompted by Dr. Elder's statement that masturbation "is a part of human sexuality and it is something that perhaps should be taught" in public schools.

16. Cited in Cameron Humphries, "Clinton's Dr. Demento," *Heterodoxy* (September 1994), 7.

17. "No Respect for Elders," *Christianity Today* (September 13, 1993), 64.

18. Ralph Reed, *Politically Incorrect* (Dallas: Word Books, 1994), 205.

19. Ibid., 205–6.

20. Ibid., 206–7.

21. Ibid., 207.

22. Ibid., 208.

23. Ibid., 209.

24. Ibid., 211.

25. Ibid.

26. Ibid., 217.

27. Ibid., 218–19.

28. Ibid., 219.

29. Rich Lowry, "Clinton's Revelation," *National Review* (March 7, 1994), 52.

30. Ibid. Carville was the director of Clinton's presidential campaign.

31. Cited in Lowry, "Clinton's Revelation," 52.

32. Ibid.

33. Ibid.

34. Ibid.

35. Ibid., 53.

36. See *Faith and Freedom* (Summer 1995), 4.

37. Mark D. Tooley, "Homosexuality Celebration at President Clinton's Church," a Special Memo from the Institute on Religion and Democracy, December 8, 1995.

38. See Mark D. Tooley, "The President's Pastor: Using a Pulpit for Politics?" *Faith and Freedom* (Spring 1995), 6–7.

39. See *Faith and Freedom* (Summer 1995), 4.

40. Tooley, "The President's Pastor," 6.

41. Ibid., 7.

Chapter Twelve: For Crying Out Loud

1. See Jim Wallis, "A Network for Renewal," *Sojourners* (July–August 1995), 6, and "Time to Organize," *Sojourners* (November–December 1995), 6–7.

2. Wallis, "A Network for Renewal," 6.

3. Ibid.

4. Ibid.

5. At least one-sixth of Wallis's long article "A Network for Renewal" was devoted to listing the newspapers and news organizations that had mentioned him and the document.

6. I have in mind here a point that I made at the end of chapter 6. It is possible that while political novices may read Wallis's language in a traditional way, his real meaning may reflect his early training in the New Left movement.

7. My quotations from the document come from an unpaginated original copy. Copies may be obtained by writing *The Cry for Renewal*, 2401 15th Street, N.W., Washington, DC 20009.

8. Dugan's comments appear as a response to a main paper in the book *No Longer Exiles: The Religious New Right in American Politics*, ed. Michael Cromartie (Washington, DC: Ethics and Public Policy Center, 1993), 82–83. Used by permission.

9. See the discussion of the Maryknoll order in chapter 2.

10. Cited in "Political Partisanship Resisted," an uncredited sidebar in *Christianity Today* (July 17, 1995), 54.

11. Ibid.

12. Richard John Neuhaus, *First Things* (November 1995), 85.

13. Ibid.

14. Ibid.

15. Ted Olsen, "Call to Renewal Alliance Divided Over Its Agenda," *Christianity Today* (April 8, 1996), 87.

16. Ibid.

17. Ibid.

18. Ibid.

19. *The Cry for Renewal* was the name of the original document. The Call to Renewal is the current name for the organization that is supposed to carry on the objectives of the document.

20. Tooley, who attended both the conference and an accompanying press conference, made these comments in a letter to the author.

21. Malden Institute Report, subtitled "Resurgence of the Religious Left" (February 13, 1996), 1–2.

22. This excerpt is from *Freedom, Justice and Hope*, edited by Marvin Olasky et al., copyright © 1988. Used by permission of Good News Publishers/Crossway Books, Wheaton, Illinois 60187. The full text, along with the names of the forty evangelicals who signed it, appears as chapter 8 in the book.

23. For an explanation and analysis of the difference between external and internal causes of poverty, see Ronald Nash, *Poverty and Wealthy: Why Socialism Doesn't Work* (Dallas: Probe Books, 1992), chap. 17. This material was also in the 1988 edition of the book published by Crossway Books.

24. This material is quoted verbatim from pages 143–44 of *Freedom, Justice and Hope*.

25. Ibid., 144–46.

26. The signers of the Villars Statement included Roberta and Howard Ahmanson (Fieldstead Institute), the late Clarence Bass (Bethel Theological Seminary), Michael Cromartie (Ethics and Public Policy Center), Lane Dennis (Crossway Books), George Grant

(evangelical author), Ken Myers (former editor, *Eternity* magazine), Udo Middleman (Francis Schaeffer Foundation), Ronald Nash, Herbert Schlossberg (author of *Idols for Destruction*), and Ted Yamamori (Food for the Hungry).

Chapter Thirteen: What You Don't Know Can Hurt You (and Others, Too)

1. The term *statism* refers to theories and actions that produce an inordinate growth in the size and power of government.

2. Benjamin Rogge, "Christian Economics: Myth or Reality?" *The Freeman* (December 1965).

3. The liberals' favorite term for Interventionism is "the mixed economy," which expresses their belief that the middle system combines the best elements of capitalism and socialism. The big weakness in such a term is the implication that there are aspects of socialism worthy to combine with anything.

4. Herbert Schlossberg, *Idols for Destruction* (Nashville: Thomas Nelson, 1983), 318.

5. Alternative terms are *voluntary* exchange versus *coerced* exchange.

6. *Capital* is a technical term that refers to anything humans can use to create wealth. Physical capital includes land, buildings, and machines. Examples of nonphysical capital are intelligence and entrepreneurial ability.

7. A full account of the reasons why interventionism fails lies beyond the scope of this book. Readers interested in more detail will find it in my books *Poverty and Wealth* (Dallas: Probe, 1992), chaps. 11–13, and *Freedom, Justice and the State* (Lanham, MD: University Press of America, 1980), chap. 5.

8. Brian Griffiths, *The Creation of Wealth* (Downers Grove, IL: InterVarsity Press, 1985), 33. Griffiths is a British evangelical whose economic expertise made him a valuable member of Prime Minister Margaret Thatcher's cabinet.

9. Peter Berger, "Underdevelopment Revisited," *Commentary* (July 1984), 41.

10. Ibid., p. 43.

11. Ibid.

12. Ibid., 45.

13. Compare this, for example, with the biblical concern for just weights and measures (Deut. 25:15–16).

14. Neither the objection nor my answer has what are sometimes called "local monopolies" in view, such as the person who happens to own the only source of water in the middle of a desert. For more on monopoly, see Ronald Nash, *Social Justice and the Christian Church* (Lanham, MD: University Press of America, 1992), 142–46, and Yale Brozen, *Is Government the Source of Monopoly? and Other Essays* (San Francisco: Cato Institute, 1980).

15. For a documentation of this claim, see Milton Friedman, *Capitalism and Freedom* (Chicago: University of Chicago Press, 1962).

16. For documentation of this claim, see Burton W. Folsom Jr., *The Myth of the Robber Barons* (Herndon, VA: Young America's Foundation, 1991). Folsom also provides examples of business ventures (such as Western railroads) that failed in spite of massive government subsidies while nonsubsidized private ventures succeeded.

17. Liberals evidence little or no interest in the fraudulent behavior of America's legislative and executive branches of government, unless the culprits belong to the other party.

18. Economist P. J. Hill of Wheaton College argues successfully that private ownership of resources is a necessary condition for effective protection of the environment. See Joseph L. Bast, Peter J. Hill, Richard C. Rue, *Eco-Sanity: A Common Sense Guide to Environmentalism* (Lanham, MD: Madison Books, 1994).

19. Readers may recall from chapter 3 that this is part of Marcuse's peculiar type of Marxism.

20. For more detailed answers to these charges, see Nash, *Freedom, Justice and the State*.

21. Arthur Shenfield, "Capitalism Under the Tests of Ethics," *Imprimis* (December 1981), no pagination.

22. Ibid.

23. Ibid.

Chapter Fourteen: Will the Real Friends of the Poor Please Stand Up?

1. See Ronald Nash, *Poverty and Wealth: Why Socialism Doesn't Work* (Dallas: Probe Books, 1992), 176–77.

2. Thomas Sowell, "The Uses of Government for Racial Equality," *National Review* (September 4, 1981), 1013.

3. James Gwartney and Thomas S. McCaleb, "Have Antipoverty Programs Increased Poverty?" *Cato Journal* 4 (Spring-Summer 1985): 15.

4. For more information regarding these numbers, see ibid., 1–16.

5. The exact figure for 1965 was 13.9 percent. While it is true that the percentage dropped still further to a low of 11.1 percent in 1973, this additional decline had little or nothing to do with War on Poverty programs, which were just getting into high gear by that time.

6. See Charles Murray, *Losing Ground: American Social Policy 1950–1980* (New York: Basic Books, 1984). In chapter 9 I referred to Campolo's positive appraisal of Murray's statistical analysis.

7. See Dwight R. Lee, "The Politics of Poverty and the Poverty of Politics," *Cato Journal* 5 (1985): 17–35.

8. *Statistical Abstract of the United States*: 1995. (Washington, DC: U.S. Bureau of the Census), 115th Edition, Sect. 12.

9. *The World Almanac and Book of Facts*, 1996 (Mahwah, NJ: Funk & Wagnalls, 1995), 139.

10. *Statistical Abstract of the United States*: 1995, Sect. 12.

11. For Murray's careful replies to his critics, see Charles Murray, "Have the Poor Been 'Losing Ground'?" *Political Science Quarterly* 100 (1985): 427–45, and Charles Murray, "How to Lie with Statistics," *National Review* (February 28, 1986), 39–41.

12. James Gwartney, "Social Progress, the Tax-Transfer Society and the Limits of Public Policy," unpublished paper, Department of Economics, Florida State University, 3.

13. Noncash benefits include such things as food stamps, school lunches, public housing, and Medicaid.

14. Loury's statements and several from other leading blacks that follow appear in a symposium, "Black American Under the Reagan Administration," *Policy Review* 35 (Fall 1985): 27–41. Loury's quote appears on page 39. Loury's mention of George Gilder is a reference to Gilder's book, *Wealth and Poverty* (New York: Basic Books, 1981).

15. Ibid., 39.

16. Ibid., 39–40.

17. Warren T. Brookes, "High Technology and Judeo-Christian Values," *Imprimis* (April 1984), no pagination.

18. Rector is a senior policy analyst at the Heritage Foundation. His report was published under the title "Is Welfare Good for Kids?" in the January 6, 1996, issue of *World* magazine, 24–25. My quotations come from the *World* article.

19. Rector, "Is Welfare Good for Kids?" *World* (January 6, 1996), 24.

20. Ibid. Rector cites experimental evidence to support his claim.

21. Ibid., 24–25.

22. Ibid., 25.

23. Ibid.

24. For an important source of additional statistics, see Robert Rector and William F. Lauber, *America's Failed $5.4 Trillion War on Poverty* (Washington, DC: Heritage Foundation, 1995).

Chapter Fifteen: Love Your Enemies (Even If They Are Conservatives)

1. Ralph Reed, president of the Coalition, states that membership is 16 percent Roman Catholic, 2 percent Jewish, 3 percent African-American, and 2 percent Hispanic, Native American, and other minorities. See Lori Sharn and Patricia Edmonds, "Religious Conservatism Reaches Out," *USA Today* (November 2, 1994), 3A. In late 1995, Reed spoke of plans for a major new outreach to Roman Catholics, who will have their own movement within the Christian Coalition called "the Catholic Alliance." Reed hopes to see the percentage of Roman Catholics in the coalition rise to 30 percent. See "Ralph Reed on Catholics," An Interview, *Crisis* (November 1995), 18–22.

2. This raises the interesting question, What is the opposite of decency, and is that what the AAUW wishes to serve as its identifying feature?

3. What, one must wonder, is the opposite of "excellence in education" and why should it be favored by an organization of university women?

4. "This Week," *National Review* (August 1, 1994), 10.

5. Gary Bauer, "Who Counts the Most Important Things of All?" *Imprimis* (July 1994), 1.

6. For the record, claims like this were always greatly oversimplified. Few of us can recall any mainline liberals helping homeless people at "rescue missions"—perhaps because of their hostility to the message of those missions. Religious conservatives in the old days supported much charity at the local level. Their accomplishments on mission fields around the world were remarkable.

7. Nathan Glazer, "Fundamentalism: A Defensive Offensive," in *Piety and Politics,* ed. Richard John Neuhaus and Michael Cromartie (Washington, DC: Ethics and Public Policy Center, 1987), 247. What Glazer calls "fundamentalism" is better understood as the kind of theological conservatism this book calls "evangelicalism."

8. Richard John Neuhaus, "What the Fundamentalists Want," in *Piety and Politics,* 5. Given the seriousness of this peril, I hasten to affirm that I am not now nor ever have been a member of the Christian Coalition.

9. Ibid.

10. You may recall from chapter 12 that this language comes from *The Cry for Renewal.* For my own views on this theory of the end-times, see Ronald Nash, *Great Divides* (Colorado Springs: NavPress, 1993), chap. 10.

11. Clifford G. Kossel, "The Moral Majority and Christian Politics," *Communio* 9 (1982): 340. The Moral Majority ceased to exist in 1989, but because the term continues to be used of people who still share some of its goals, Kossel's comments can apply to them.

12. Ibid.

13. Robert Zwier, *Born-Again Politics* (Downers Grove, IL: InterVarsity Press, 1982), 99.

14. In the 1990s, the pejorative connotations have been extended to the word "evangelical" as well.

15. Neuhaus, "What the Fundamentalists Want," in *Piety and Politics,* 12.

16. See Glazer, "Fundamentalism," 247.

17. Ibid., 250.

18. Glazer usually uses the term "fundamentalism," unaware as he seems to be of the subtle yet important differences between fundamentalists and evangelicals. I have substituted the more general terms "evangelical" and "evangelicalism." For a discussion of the differences, see Ronald Nash, *Evangelicals in America* (Nashville: Abingdon Press, 1987), chap. 5.

19. Glazer, "Fundamentalism."

20. Ibid., 251.

21. Ibid., 245.

22. Ralph Reed, *Politically Incorrect* (Dallas: Word, 1994), 72.

23. Ibid.

24. Ibid., 73.

25. Cited by Michael Cromartie in *Disciples and Democracy,* ed. Michael Cromartie (Washington, DC: Ethics and Public Policy Center, 1994), xiii.

26. Ibid., 54. Reed gives the sources for his quotes on p. 273.

27. Ibid.

28. See "Ralph Reed on Catholics," An Interview, *Crisis* (November 1995), 19.

29. Ibid., 20.

30. See ibid.

31. See Reed, *Politically Incorrect,* 9ff.

32. Ibid., 59–60.

33. Ibid., 9.

34. Ibid.

35. Ibid. Reed's last sentence appears to be directed at the "flaming rhetoric and name-calling" of people in the religious Left.

36. Reed, *Politically Incorrect*, 24.

37. Ibid., 71.

38. "Ralph Reed on Catholics," 22.

39. Michael Cromartie, "Listening to Mr. Right," A Conversation with William F. Buckley Jr., *Christianity Today* (October 2, 1995), 36–37.